I0817212

# AT HOME IN CORNWALL

## SECRETS OF CORNISH COUNTRY HOUSE STYLE

KATY & MILO CAMPBELL

Photography by MARK NICHOLSON

ABRAMS, NEW YORK

# CONTENTS

# CORNWALL, "THE DELECTABLE DUCHY" AN INTRODUCTION

Sir John Betjeman, poet laureate and adopted Cornishman, maintained that Cornwall was more than just an outpost of England—"It is not another county, but another country." He was not alone in feeling this. The historian Sir Simon Jenkins describes Cornwall as "a land beyond England." Its sense of otherness comes primarily from its geography. The Cornish peninsula, which is both the most southerly and westerly corner of the British Isles, protrudes into the sea as a jutting seventy-five-mile-long promontory. It has more coastline than any other county and is surrounded by the wild Atlantic Ocean to the north and the more sheltered waters of the English Channel to the south. No Cornish village is further than sixteen miles from the sea and there is a briny savour to the air wherever you are. It has an island feel because that is almost what it is. Not only is it bordered on three sides by the sea, but it is separated from Devon and the rest of England by the great River Tamar. Apart from a tiny strip of land near the hamlet of Woolley, it is impossible to reach Cornwall without crossing water. And once you do, everything changes.

Cornwall has a temperate climate influenced by the balmy air and warm water brought across the Atlantic by the Gulf Stream. It is sunnier than the rest of the United Kingdom and exotic subtropical plants grow here—even palm trees and citrus fruit. And it is beautiful—a land of dramatic cliffs sprinkled with sea pinks, sandy coves, hidden valleys, and rolling moors clad in purple heather. Its beauty is often rugged, just like its people—hardy souls who traditionally led dangerous, physical lives as miners and fishermen.

Cornish people are a breed apart. They are a recognised ethnic group with their own language, which was wholly prevalent up until the eighteenth century. Their tough, brave, and independent spirit can be sensed in the unofficial Cornish national anthem "Trelawny," which is often sung with patriotic fervour at rugby matches:

A good sword and a trusty hand!
A merry heart and true!
King James's men shall understand
What Cornish lads can do!

**PAGE 1:** A circular, grotto-style terrace overlooking the mouth of Fowey Harbour

**PAGE 2:** An Edwardian garden room overlooking St Austell Bay

**PAGES 3–4:** Art Deco furniture in a bedroom of Point Neptune House

**OPPOSITE:** Clifftop houses above Daymer Bay in Trebertherick

**ABOVE:** An old fisherman's cottage in the tiny medieval harbour of Port Quin

**OPPOSITE:** Rock Beach in the Camel Estuary

Cornish miners, who dug for tin and copper, were as hard as the granite they tackled, and their leisure time revolved around Cornish wrestling (which calls for immense endurance and strength) and "purring"—a horrendous-sounding sport whose contestants were forbidden the use of their hands but would kick each other with their iron-shod miners' boots. The other main industry was fishing, most commonly for pilchards, whose shoals could be spotted from clifftops as purple shadows on the blue-green of the sea. These twin professions gave rise to the traditional Cornish toast of "Fish, tin, and copper!"

There is also a dark side to the Cornish character. Cornwall was once famous for its pirates and smugglers, and wrecking was more than just a nefarious pursuit but an established enterprise. Today, the Cornish economy depends heavily on tourism. It is the most popular holiday destination within the UK, with more than five million visitors every year. They are drawn by its outstanding natural beauty and also its culture.

This is a land of ghost stories and pagan superstitions, all springing from a history in which fact and fable seem irretrievably blurred. It is certainly an ancient place. Cornwall is littered with neolithic henges, burial sites, and hearths

dating back as far as five thousand years before the birth of Christ. Speaking of whom, one early legend has it that Jesus visited Cornwall as a boy, travelling with his uncle Joseph of Arimathea, who was a tin merchant. They are said to have landed at what is now St. Just in Roseland (described by Betjeman as "the most beautiful churchyard on earth"). This story is supposed to have inspired William Blake's iconic hymn "Jerusalem," whose opening lines ask, "And did those feet in ancient time, walk upon England's mountains green?" Cornwall is also steeped in Arthurian legend. The ruined castle of Tintagel was named by the twelfth-century writer Geoffrey of Monmouth as the place where King Arthur was conceived.

Writers have often found themselves drawn to and bewitched by Cornwall. In the 1920s, Virginia Woolf, whilst lying in bed and listening to the waves, described feeling "the purest ecstasy I can conceive." "Why am I so incredibly and incurably romantic about Cornwall?" she asked herself. Her friend D. H. Lawrence was similarly afflicted and felt on his arrival in Cornwall that he had entered "the Promised Land" and discovered "a new continent of the soul." The county has produced plenty of homegrown talent, most notably William Golding, Daphne du Maurier, and the folklorist and historian Sir Arthur Quiller-Couch, who coined the term "The Delectable Duchy." Artists abound as well, many of them enraptured by the soft Cornish light. St. Ives has given its name to a school of famous names including Ben Nicholson, Barbara Hepworth, Patrick Heron, Terry Frost, and many more. Before them, in the nineteenth century, J.M.W. Turner painted around St. Ives and claimed, "I have never seen so many natural beauties in such a limited spot as I have seen here."

After the architectural historian Nikolaus Pevsner completed his 1951 survey of the buildings of Cornwall, he wrote, in a typically dour manner, "The county has more to reward the picturesque traveller than the architectural scholar." But he continued, "Although Cornwall possesses little of the highest aesthetic quality there is much that is lovable and much that is moving." Leaving strict architectural arguments aside, he was certainly correct about the charm of so many Cornish houses. This book aims to provide a sense of their captivating loveliness. There are a broad range of houses within these pages, from the most modest of cottages to the grandest of stately homes. There are pleasure palaces and castles next to more utilitarian buildings. Some are ancient and some are modern, but all are intertwined with the extraordinary landscape in which they sit and all, I hope you will agree, are utterly enchanting.

**OPPOSITE ABOVE:** The lighthouse on Trevose Head, built in 1847 as a guide for vessels in the Bristol Channel

**OPPOSITE BELOW:** A coast guard hut on Mawgan Porth Beach

**OVERLEAF:** Sunset at Fistral Beach in Newquay

# *The* HOUSES

# Antony
## *The stateliest of homes*

As you wander through Antony's grand interlinked staterooms, as thousands of visitors do every year, you are met by the unblinking stares of generations of the Carew family, looking down from their gilded frames. But dotted about on the tables beneath these historic oil paintings are more contemporary portraits—photographic ones. For the Carews, who have lived on this spot for more than six hundred years, still reside here to this day and, unusually for a National Trust house, are very much in evidence. You sense them in the half-finished puzzle in the library, a discarded coffee cup on the mantel shelf in the hall, a foam Nerf gun bullet lost under a table in the saloon. You might smell their cooked breakfast or even bump into the inhabitants themselves, because Antony is still a much-loved family home, which adds hugely to its charm.

Sir John Carew Pole gave the house and formal gardens into the care of the National Trust in 1961 on the understanding that the family could continue to reside there. Today, his grandson Tremayne Carew Pole lives there with his young family. It is an unusual dynamic that sees the family going about their lives under the partial scrutiny of the paying visitors to the house. Tremayne admits that it is an odd thing, but he is used to it. He remembers as a child brushing past old ladies as he climbed the stairs in his wet swimming trunks, fresh from a dip in the sea. Tremayne's own children are always taking their dogs into the library and talking to the guests. They act as unofficial tour guides, giving their, as Tremayne puts it, "questionable" versions of the history of the house. Visitors even tramp round Tremayne's bedroom. "Which means I have to be fairly tidy and make my bed in the morning," he says. "Visitors are always examining the books on my bedside table. It makes you slightly self-aware, lest you be caught out reading something terribly lowbrow."

Antony is a Grade I listed house, faced in fine Pentewan stone, which glows silvery grey in the evening sun from its position high above the River Lynher. There has been a Carew property here since the late fifteenth century, but the

The front façade of Antony, completed in 1721

The view from the entrance of the house

**OPPOSITE ABOVE:** A recently restored eighteenth-century dovecote

**OPPOSITE BELOW:** The bronze water feature on the west lawn, which reflects the conical yew hedge behind, is by sculptor William Pye.

house as it now stands was built by Sir William Carew in 1711. As an example of Queen Anne architecture, it is, according to the architectural historian Nikolai Pevsner, "without doubt the best example of its date in Cornwall." The north façade is of two storeys and nine bays, with the central three bays stressed by a pediment. With the exception of the architrave, it is almost austere in its lack of decoration. But it is supremely elegant in its composition and proportions.

Inside is an eclectic mix of furniture. Some came from the previous Tudor-era house that stood here, and some was bought or commissioned at the same time as the house was built. The reception rooms on the ground floor give a glimpse into generations of aristocratic Cornish life. A portrait of Richard Carew (who was a contemporary of Shakespeare) hangs in the hall. Richard was author of *The Survey of Cornwall* (1602), an unrivalled portrait of the county in Elizabethan times, covering everything from the rules of Cornish wrestling to the best way to pickle a pilchard. A ship's bell from 1622 dredged from Portsmouth Harbour sits underneath a table in the hall. It is an appropriate object for a house which, along with the ancient parish where it lies, is said to be named for St. Anthony, venerated all over the world as the patron saint of lost articles.

The house has sweeping views over a Humphry Repton–designed landscape and a series of beautiful gardens. During high summer the family escape to "The Bothy"—a walled garden hidden away from the public where there is a pool, a tennis court, and a croquet lawn. The children like to catch crabs on the muddy beach of the river at the bottom of the garden.

On the day we visit, we sit with Tremayne in the library, which is his favourite room in the house. It is dominated by a portrait of Alexander Carew in a red-trimmed jerkin, painted in 1643. Tremayne's great-grandmother had the jerkin copied, and there is a photograph of Tremayne wearing it as a boy beneath the portrait. Alexander was a Parliamentarian during the English Civil War and was made governor of the strategically important Drake's Island in Plymouth Sound. However, when the tide of war seemed to be changing in the king's direction, Alexander attempted to switch sides and join the Royalists. It didn't work out, and he was arrested by Cromwell's forces on the island's beach and shipped off to London for trial and was subsequently executed. His own family was so disgusted by his betrayal that they cut his portrait out of its frame, rolled it up, and hid it in the stables. It was replaced only after the Restoration, and to this day you can see the stitching at the bottom of the painting where it was cut. In contrast, Alexander's half brother John never wavered in his parliamentary zeal. He was one of those who signed Charles I's death warrant. After the Restoration, he stood trial for treason and was executed. Two brothers, divided by their loyalties and each executed, one by each side.

**ABOVE:** Tremayne Carew Pole sitting beneath his forebears in the library at Antony. It is his favourite room in the house.

**LEFT:** Most of the furniture in the saloon is of the time of the building of the house. However, some of the paintings come by way of Tremayne's great-great-grandmother, who was a sister of J. P. Morgan.

**ABOVE:** The library is the family's favourite room in the house, particularly in winter, and is the scene of much game playing.

**OPPOSITE:** Charles I looks down from his portrait above the fireplace in the hall. The picture was painted at his trial in 1648, one month before his execution.

I ask our host about his own name—Tremayne Carew Pole is somewhat distinctive. "Tremayne is a Cornish name but not one particularly connected to the Carew Pole family. My father just liked it. He wanted to call my younger brother Piran (the patron saint of Cornwall), but my mother said you've already got one son with a silly Cornish name, so they ended up calling him Johnny." The family name was Pole-Carew from the 1740s until the early twentieth century. But when Tremayne's grandfather inherited the Pole baronetcy (from his seventh cousin), he switched the order to Carew Pole. I had heard that this began a tradition whereby the family would swap its name with every new generation. Tremayne laughs at the myth and says he has no intention of reversing the order. What he does intend to do though is tidy up the game of Twister that his children have left out on the library floor, before the next batch of visitors arrive.

**ABOVE:** Dominating the library is a portrait of Alexander Carew in a red-trimmed jerkin, painted in 1643. Tremayne's grandmother had the jerkin copied, and there is a photograph of Tremayne wearing it as a boy beneath the portrait. It's still possible to see the stitching at the bottom of the picture from when it was cut out of its frame by Alexander's own family, disgusted by his betrayal during the English Civil War.

**OPPOSITE:** Tremayne's dachshund, Treacle, making itself comfortable in the library

**ABOVE:** The Green Bedroom has views over parkland to the River Lynher below the house. Outside the bedroom hangs a portrait of Rachel Carew—the inspiration behind Daphne du Maurier's novel *My Cousin Rachel*.

**OPPOSITE:** Jemima and Lucien's playroom on the lower ground floor of the house. Its walls are adorned with antique hunting trophies.

A calming green-panelled bathroom on the first floor of the house

**LEFT:** The family kitchen—which is not open to the public—adorned with rosettes won by Jemima Carew Pole at Pony Club

**OPPOSITE:** The kitchen is decorated with bespoke tiles featuring "all the things we can see from the window," including the family's ponies, Merlin, Po, and Dancer.

ANTONY
COOKING
THE PIG
OTTOLENGHI SIMPLE
CORONATION

The delightful symmetry of Antony's Queen Anne–style façade

# The Stewardry
## *On the Boconnoc estate*

The ancient estate of Boconnoc has been the family home of three of England's greatest prime ministers. It was purchased in 1717 by Thomas Pitt, Governor of Fort St. George in Madras, with the proceeds of the sale of one of the most famous diamonds in the world. The Regent Diamond (also known as the Pitt Diamond) was cut by Thomas into a flawless 141-carat diamond of unsurpassed brilliance. He sold it to the royal family of France, where, in turn, it was set into the coronation crown of Louis XV, used to adorn a hat worn by Marie Antoinette, and mounted on Napoleon Bonaparte's sword guard. Today it resides in the Louvre Museum.

The Pitt family went on to great things, producing two prime ministers, and Boconnoc was eventually inherited by Anne Pitt. Anne married William Grenville, the prime minister who abolished slavery in the early nineteenth century. When Anne and William both died, William's nephew, a Fortescue, inherited the estate. And it is the Fortescue family who remain here to this day.

Boconnoc is a captivating estate littered with treasures that include, amongst others, a fifteenth-century church with King Charles I's coat of arms and a letter from the monarch thanking Cornwall for its support during the English Civil War, a Georgian bathhouse with a myrtle bush at its entrance planted from Queen Victoria's wedding bouquet, a stable yard designed by Sir John Soane, the oldest cricket pavilion in Cornwall, and gardens abundant with exotic subtropical flora. But one of Boconnoc's greatest jewels is the Stewardry—home to Sarah Fortescue and her family.

The house was originally a vicarage before becoming the home of the steward (or land agent) of the estate. A continuous line of agents lived there until the 1950s, when Sarah's grandparents moved in and it became her father's childhood home. It overlooks the River Lerryn and the surrounding ancient woodland. The house has a seventeenth-century core but a very pretty Georgian wing. When Sarah moved in it had been largely untouched for half a century, and Sarah, as a professional interior designer, relished the challenge of redecorating it.

The eighteenth-century front façade of the Stewardry

We enter the house into a large hall used as a dining room. The room is dominated by a square table on which sits a brass bucket containing spring flowers from the garden. These purple, pink, and red blooms are electrifyingly colourful. Their vibrancy is reflected by the pictures on the wall, all painted by artist friends of Sarah's. Sarah likes to use colour, pattern, and texture to create harmonious interiors. "I am ignited within by colour," she says, a passion which partly comes from having lived and travelled extensively in India and Africa, and you sense it throughout the house, from the bright Maasai blankets in her son's bedroom to the bespoke pink in the anteroom to the drawing room, which Sarah created herself by mixing a dark plum with ochre and white to produce the coral colour that she wanted. When decorating her own home, a key tenet was "to try and bring the outside in" and this is evident in many of the rooms, from the calming greens of her bedroom to the wallpaper in the drawing room, which Sarah designed herself, inspired by flowers from the garden.

And what an "outside" it is. The Boconnoc estate dates to the fourteenth century, but its deer park is even earlier and is mentioned in the Domesday Book. Its lands used to stretch from the north coast to the south coast and, until the 1960s, included the Watch House—a nineteenth-century lookout used for spotting shoals of pilchards (an activity familiar to all *Poldark* fans). It is the only building on a seven-mile stretch of cliffs between Polruan and Polperro. The estate is now a fraction of its former size, but its parkland alone still extends to seven hundred acres. The early eighteenth-century house that Thomas Pitt built is a handsome L-shaped building. It was used as a base by the Americans in World War II and then fell into a derelict state over the next forty years. Sarah's late father, Anthony, inherited it in 1996. At that time the only inhabitant of the house was a barn owl. Anthony and his wife, Elizabeth, were determined to restore the house to its former glory and embarked on a twelve-year project to do just that. On its completion, in 2012, the house received the Historic Houses/Sotheby's Restoration Award, and, in the same year, the Georgian Group Architectural Award for the restoration of the painted staircase. It was Anthony's dream for the Fortescue family to live there once more but the realities of living in such a large house meant that it has instead become the centre of Elizabeth's thriving events business.

Sarah and her five-year-old son, Max, appreciate how special it is to grow up amongst Boconnoc's ancient woodlands. "It is a haven, and a utopia, and the stars at night are a delight," says Sarah. Their days are filled with den seeking and "game drives" to watch the fallow deer in the park surrounding the cricket pitch. On a recent summer's afternoon, Sarah and Max stopped by the lake to watch a heron attacking an adder. "It would dive down to get hold of the snake,

**OPPOSITE:** All the paintings in the dining hall are by artist friends of Sarah's. The picture hanging on the left is of nearby Lantic Bay, painted by Cornish artist Wendy Rolt, who is known for her bold abstract landscapes.

**ABOVE:** Antique leather-topped desk whose lamps have shades by Sarah Fortescue Designs. The curtains are made with a Mulberry fabric.

**OPPOSITE AND OVERLEAF:** Sarah designed the wallpaper in the drawing room herself. She wanted to "bring the outside in" and reflect the gardens outside the windows of the room, hence the magnolia and carnelians on an emerald background.

which would then wrap itself tightly around the beak, causing the heron to let go. The process went on repeat for a quarter of an hour until the heron gave up and the adder slid away, unconquered."

Before we leave Boconnoc, Max accompanies us on a stroll along the "Stewardry Walk." The flowers are incredible, but Sarah draws our attention to the lichen: "Experts from all over the world come to study it. It is proof of the purity of the air here." After a few hundred yards, we stumble across "Lady Hamilton's bath"—a marble tub, sitting in a clearing, once used by Admiral Lord Nelson's mistress—another historic treasure in this most magical of estates.

SECRET GARDENERS
WOOD

**ABOVE:** Sarah Fortescue in her drawing room, whose walls are covered in a paper of her own design

**OPPOSITE:** The anteroom to the drawing room is also used as an occasional breakfast room. The chairs were made by Sarah's father, Anthony Fortescue. The walls are painted in a bespoke pink, which Sarah mixed herself. She started with a dark plum, adding ochre and white, and applied the scumble glaze to create the tonal, coral colour that she wanted.

**LEFT:** In this guest bedroom the headboards are covered in a material from Schumacher, the cube stool was handmade in Cornwall, and the curtain fabric was brought back from South Africa.

**OPPOSITE ABOVE:** In Sarah's bedroom, the curtains are made with Angel Ferns from Sanderson. The Gustavian commodes come from Lorfords Antiques in the Cotswolds, on which stand lamps and shades from Pooky Lighting. The walls are painted Acorn by Little Greene. Sarah wanted her bedroom to be elegant and serene. "There is something very calming about green and white."

**OPPOSITE BELOW:** The beds in Max's room are covered in brightly coloured Maasai blankets from Kenya. The headboards are covered in a Pierre Frey fabric. The lampshade is by Sarah Fortescue Designs. The curtain tassels are by Samuel & Sons. The walls are painted in a striking blue by Benjamin Moore.

**ABOVE:** Sarah Fortescue and her son, Max, aged four

**RIGHT:** The east-facing façade of Boconnoc—built in 1721 by Thomas Pitt

# Bokelly
## *The gardener's house*

Basking in the warmth of the Gulf Stream, Cornwall boasts some of the most diverse and beautiful gardens in the entire British Isles, gardens that are packed with native flora as well as exotic plants and trees from all over the world, which thrive in the subtropical climate. Most of the great gardens of the county—with magical names like Trebah, Glendurgan, Caerhays, Tregrehan, and the Lost Gardens of Heligan—are found on the South Coast, where the climate is gentler and it is less windy. Bokelly, however, is in St. Kew, three miles inland from Port Isaac on the North Coast. Its owner, Henrietta Courtauld, would have loved to have a house on the coast itself, but she needed a garden, and being on a clifftop is too unforgiving. Plus, as she says, "I do love the Cornwall countryside—particularly the hedgerows in spring when they are heaving with wild garlic, primroses, wood anemones, and bluebells."

Gardening is not only Henrietta's passion but also her profession. She was originally a lawyer but was soon diverted by her love of horticulture and moved into garden design, working with Tom Stuart-Smith for many years. Then, in 2012, she teamed up with her old friend Bridget Elworthy and set up the Land Gardeners. Together they designed gardens and grew cut flowers, based at Bridget's then home of Wardington Manor in Oxfordshire. Over time the pair grew more and more interested in soil health and creating biodiverse gardens, and recently they "jumped the garden wall" and started working with farmers—trialling methods of feeding soil on farms without chemicals. They have also authored two bestselling books. The latest—*Soil to Table*—combines their reflections on soil health and growing food, with delicious recipes by Lulu Cox.

So, when Henrietta and her husband, Toby, were looking for a house in Cornwall, the ability to create wonderful gardens around it was of paramount importance. They ended up buying Bokelly, an historic house surrounded by eleven acres of verdant land. Bokelly was the ancient seat of the Bokelly family, a notable Cornish dynasty. John de Bokelly was the Member of Parliament for

The family entrance into the house is via the kitchen wing, which was built in the early nineteenth century.

Henrietta collecting rhubarb (which the family like to eat as a compote for breakfast) from her walled kitchen garden

Helston in 1343, and Nicholas Bokelly was the MP for Bodmin in 1448. It later became the residence of the Carnsew family. Surviving fragments of William Carnsew's diary for 1576–77 provide not only a rare insight into the life of the justice of the peace and his mining ventures but also interesting references to Bokelly. The Carnsews rebuilt the house in the seventeenth century (c.1615), but some fragments of an earlier house still remain, including a medieval window high in the northeast wall of the building. Like all historic houses, it was then altered and remodelled over the years, and the kitchen range was added sometime in the nineteenth century. The current drawing room is the oldest part of the house and would have been a Cornish long room.

Henrietta and Toby bought the house eighteen years ago when their three children, Willow, Lilac, and August were toddlers. Henrietta set to work outside immediately and has created a series of informal gardens that come into their own at different times of the year. Although they are private, she has opened them up for the National Garden Scheme. The most recently planted part of the garden is the walled kitchen garden.

Henrietta professes not to be a great cook ("I burn things a lot"), but she uses all manner of glorious produce from this plot, including rhubarb, chives, borage, fennel, courgettes, flat-leaf parsley, lettuces, French beans, angelica, cavalo nero, artichokes, and, of course, edible flowers like calendula and nasturtium. And her orchard contains gooseberries, blackberries, figs, and Kea plums (which are similar to Damsons and are unique to Cornwall). She also has a dedicated cutting garden where she grows flowers for the house.

Bokelly is full of flowers, both real and in artistic form in prints and paintings, as well as in floral fabrics and wallpapers. On the day that we visit, the house is brimming with evocatively named roses, including Jude the Obscure, Lark Ascending, Queen of Sweden, and Constance Spry. The drawing room is decorated with delphiniums, and there is a profusion of pelargoniums on the porch, as well as huge sprigs of apple mint in the kitchen. There is an abundance of butterflies as well. "A garden only really starts to hum if it is full of butterflies, insects, and birds," says Henrietta. "We need to encourage them by creating as much diversity as possible in our gardens and letting areas of grass grow long. We shouldn't all aspire to have acres of tightly cropped lawns but should leave things wilder. It's better for us and the planet, and makes gardens seem more alive." The house is also full of incredible wallpapers, all by Marthe Armitage. Henrietta is a huge fan and has visited her studio to watch how she designs her papers and then prints them by hand. "I love her designs because they are so playful and full of movement," she says, "and you can pick the colours yourself."

A prettily painted bench on the south lawn

One room in the house stands out from all the others, as it is covered with dozens of framed nautical charts. This is Toby's study. He is a keen sailor who keeps a boat in Mylor, high in the Fal Estuary. It is a Southerly yacht with a variable draft swing keel that means it can be sailed in shallow waters. The whole family likes going out on it, but Henrietta's sea legs aren't as sturdy as her husband's. "I like the soil. He likes the sea."

As we prepare to leave this Cornish Eden, Henrietta hands us a bottle of the Land Gardener's "tipple"—a medicinal nonalcoholic brew made of apple cider vinegar, hedgerow berries, hawthorn, and all manner of herbs. She explains that a daily shot is excellent for good gut health, and we all need to look after our bodies as well as the soil. Yeghes da! (As the Cornish say—good health!)

**ABOVE:** Pelargoniums on the porch and a croquet set for games on the lawn

**LEFT:** Henrietta with her newly built greenhouse

**ABOVE:** The curtains in the Flower Room are Fez Stripe by Lulu Lytle of Soane (who is a friend of Henrietta's). The pictures are old table mats designed in the 1960s by various St. Ives artists and produced by Heal's.

**RIGHT:** The cupboards in the kitchen are topped with local Delabole slate. Henrietta installed the AGA, which is "Cornish clotted cream" in colour, with white tiles behind. The wallpaper is Butterflies by Marthe Armitage.

**ABOVE:** The garden chairs in the hall ("a complete flight of fancy") are part of a set that Henrietta found on the Pimlico Road and painted yellow. The pictures are painted by Emma Tennant.

**LEFT:** The huge fireplace in the drawing room contains an ancient bread oven, which is still occasionally used by the Courtaulds for making pizzas. The pegs above the mantel shelf were originally used for oars. The wallpaper is Tobacco Plant by Marthe Armitage. The covers on the cushions on the two armchairs were made by Henrietta, who cut them from an old tablecloth. The flowers on the side table are delphiniums and Cephalaria gigantea.

**OPPOSITE ABOVE:** The Pagoda Bedroom is named after its wallpaper with motifs of clematis and Chinese pagodas. It is a nod to Toby, who was brought up in Hong Kong. The bed has a cane chinoiserie headboard.

**OPPOSITE BELOW:** Henrietta's bedroom is painted in Coral I from Paint & Paper Library. The 1695 map of Cornwall features Bokelly and was given to her by her friend the designer Lulu Lytle.

**ABOVE:** Willow's bedroom is painted in Coral II from Paint & Paper Library. It has a zinc desk. The seaweed prints were a gift from Charlie McCormick, and the curtains are from Lewis & Wood.

**ABOVE:** The front of Bokelly, which dates back to the early seventeenth century

**RIGHT:** The old threshing barn in the garden is Grade II* and dates back to the 1500s.

# Constantine Cottage
## *The Queen of Constantine Bay*

The parish of St. Merryn, crowned by the headland of Trevose, is famous for its seven sandy beaches, known locally as the "seven bays for seven days." Porthcothan, Treyarnon, Booby's, Constantine, Mother Ivey's, Harlyn, and Trevone—I love their idiosyncratic names. All are delightful, and everyone who lives by, or visits, this stretch of coast has their favourite one. Mine is Constantine Bay—a sweeping arc of more than half a mile of soft, golden sand. It is popular with surfers and families alike, and at low tide it is excellent for rock-pooling. Constantine is not only outstandingly scenic but also a designated Site of Special Scientific Interest because of its extensive sand dunes.

The bay is thought to be named after an obscure Cornish saint, Constantine, who one legend has it was a nephew of King Arthur and was an acolyte of Saint Petroc. He was a wealthy man who supposedly converted to Christianity after an incident deer hunting. Taking refuge from a sudden storm, Constantine found himself joined in his shelter by the stag he had been pursuing, provoking in him a damascene conversion. The local church is dedicated to him, and a feast day is still celebrated in his name on the nearest Sunday to March 9. William Peter, a nineteenth-century Cornish Member of Parliament, records attending one feast day in his book *The Parochial History of Cornwall.* He describes it being marked by a hurling match (a sort of Gaelic lacrosse) followed by the eating of a special pie made of limpets and raisins.

Sitting proudly on a clifftop at the southern end of the bay is a lone house, accessed by a sandy track. Constantine Cottage is undoubtedly the queen of Constantine Bay. Her enviable position gives her commanding views over the entire crescent beach and onto Trevose Head. She was built in 1824 as a fisherman's cottage and is now owned by Martin and Amanda Hedley. Amanda has known the house her entire life. Her mother used to stay here in the 1930s with the glamourous family who then owned it. She and her friends would sometimes fly down from London after a party, still in their black tie, and land

Constantine Cottage on its clifftop overlooking Constantine Bay

in a field behind the house. When Amanda and Martin bought the cottage, as a holiday home, forty years ago, it was a tiny and relatively humble abode. As their children grew up and produced children of their own, Amanda decided to extend and reconfigure the house to make it more comfortable for them all. She hired designer and interior decorator Paolo Moschino to help with the project. The Hedleys received planning permission to extend the house at the back to create a large and airy open-plan kitchen, dining, and living space. The floors were lowered on the ground floor and the ceilings raised on the first floor to create space and light. In terms of decoration, Paolo decided to embrace the sea, and so the whole house is painted in blues and whites. Nautical stripes abound, and everywhere you look there are maritime references, from lamps shaped like lighthouses and shells to models of sailors and vintage photographs of yachts. He even designed Martin's dressing room to look like a ship's cabin.

Amanda has always loved the sea. She grew up near Chichester Harbour and learnt to sail as a child. Her grandfather Noel Van Raalte used to race powerboats and once owned Brownsea Island off Poole Harbour. Amanda derives immense joy from being either in or on the water and swims in Constantine Bay every morning. Martin is a "landlubber" by comparison but has learnt to love the sea as well. Their life, during the six months of the year they spend at Constantine Cottage, sounds blissful. Much of it, of course, revolves around the beach. They forage for mussels and sea herbs and use hooks to catch edible crabs from the rock pools. They always come back for lunch, as it seems pointless to sit on a rock picnicking when you can sit above the sea in their beautiful lawned garden and enjoy the view in comfort. Although sometimes for fun they have a BBQ on the sand, and Amanda lowers buckets full of food and drink on a rope down to the beach below. They sometimes walk to Padstow for lunch or go out for dinner at the PIG hotel in Harlyn Bay (where there is now an excellent lobster shack). Occasionally they visit Martha Prideaux-Brune (who is Amanda's goddaughter) in the Prideaux Walled Garden in Padstow, where Martha hosts drinks parties on Friday evenings. From time to time, they take the ferry from Padstow across the Camel Estuary to "the Dark Side" (as Martin jokingly calls Rock) to water-ski or visit friends and have lunch at the Mariners pub. The Hedleys are also keen but amateurish golfers who love to hack round the Trevose golf course. The club there was founded in 1925 and is known as one of the finest links courses in the country.

Their grandchildren come to stay constantly. Jack, aged eleven, is in residence on the day we visit. He likes to spend all day on the beach, surfing, playing cricket, and "sand-duning" (sliding down the dunes on his surfboard). Jack boasts that "Granny is an amazing cook" who makes him delicious baked eggs,

The view from the house of Constantine Bay, looking towards Trevose Head

"the best" chocolate mousse, and fabulous jellies. His grandfather sometimes gives him and his brother pocket money to go and buy hot chocolate from the coffee shack at the entrance to the beach. Amanda says that they can watch the children on the beach from the garden, which means that they can let them explore freely. It is an ideal family setup.

The Sunday before we came, the Hedleys hosted a lunch for twenty-eight people in the garden. Sitting at trestle tables, they tucked into a feast of crab and lobsters caught in pots just a few hundred yards off the bay. Lunch continued into the evening, and as the setting sun lit up the clifftop house, the assembled group toasted the queen of Constantine Bay.

TIFFANY&CO.
OF THE SEA

**ABOVE:** A nautical portrait in a corner of the sitting room

**LEFT.** Antique French prints of shells in mirrored frames hang on the wall of the sitting room. The tiny fireplace has a slate-topped surround for sitting on.

**ABOVE:** The sitting-room end of the open-plan kitchen. The desk is from Petworth Antiques Market. The big lamps on the desk came from a decorative fair in Battersea.

**RIGHT:** A zinc-topped dining table sits on a striped rug in the open-plan kitchen. The shell lamps on the sideboard are from Paolo Moschino. The entire room is painted in a nautical blue and white (paint from Dulux).

**LEFT:** A view from the kitchen door onto the clifftop garden with the beach beyond

**Above:** The bay window in the sitting room is home to Amanda's collection of lighthouse lamps.

**ABOVE:** Above the headboards in the Brown Bedroom is a portrait of Amanda, aged seven, painted by Anthony Devas.

**ABOVE RIGHT:** The luggage in the upstairs landing belonged to Amanda's family (her maiden name was Russell). The portrait above is a pastel of Amanda's mother.

The blue-and-white nautical theme continues into Amanda's bedroom. The striped walls are painted rather than papered. Even the teddy bears are wearing naval jumpers. The desk, which has been repurposed as a dressing table, belonged to Amanda's mother. Amanda painted it white.

**ABOVE:** Martin's cabin-like dressing room was designed by Paolo Moschino with porthole details. The landscape painting above the berth is of Constantine Bay.

**OPPOSITE:** The striped chair in the kitchen came from Ralph Lauren in New York.

**ABOVE:** Amanda in her garden overlooking Constantine Bay. The rocky outcrop off Trevose Head is known as the Bull.

**RIGHT:** Constantine Cottage, built in 1824 as a fisherman's cottage

# Fentafriddle
## *A farm with a view*

Fentafriddle is a farm with a view, and not just any view. This clifftop plot of forty-five acres with an historic farmhouse in the middle has, according to *Country Life*, "the kind of views over the Atlantic Ocean that seem to expand beyond the horizon and into space itself." It was in the pages of that august magazine that Emma Dean and her husband, David, first spotted Fentafriddle. This was during the first COVID-19 lockdown, in March 2020, and they were sitting in their house in Clapham dreaming, like so many others, of escaping from London. As soon as the lockdown was lifted, they booked to view it and raced down from London, agog with excitement. But when they arrived and drove up the driveway, it was grey and misty. "The owners kept saying that the view was amazing, but it was raining so hard that we couldn't see the sea," says Emma. "We loved the house but left feeling underwhelmed." The Deans went for a slightly despondent lunch nearby before heading back to London. But that afternoon the clouds parted, and the sun came out, and they asked whether they could go back for another look. Standing in the field in front of the farm, they could not only see far out to sea but also look north along the coast to the ruins of Tintagel Castle—a mystical place attached to the legend of King Arthur. "As soon as we saw the view, we were sold."

It took seven months to complete the mortgage paperwork because of the post-lockdown boom. This turned out to be an accidental positive, as it meant there was plenty of time for planning. And so, on the same day that the Deans got the keys, the builders moved in and started on an overhaul of the house.

The outside of historic Fentafriddle Farmhouse

**ABOVE:** Emma Dean standing in the doorway of Fentafriddle Farmhouse with two of the finest Labradors in Cornwall

**OPPOSITE:** The kitchen terrace has fabulous views straight out to sea. Emma says that it is important to have metal furniture as the salt air devours wooden furniture very quickly. The table and chairs were a bespoke design by James Fuller from Home and Garden Ironwork.

Emma wanted to decorate the house herself; however, being on maternity leave and looking after two small boys and a baby whilst managing the farm remotely, she felt she needed a bit of help. So she partnered with interior designer Isabelle Lomas, "who was very game for taking on a client who wanted to be so hands on." Together they created a house that is utterly delightful and perfectly balanced. It is a house that seems completely at ease with itself and retains the feeling of a traditional Cornish farmhouse whilst being layered with modern and contemporary art, furniture, and fabrics.

The house is in an idyllic setting. Its rolling farmland is mostly used as grazing for North Devon cattle—also known as Red Devons because of their deep red colour. They produce excellent beef after munching on the verdant grass whilst staring out to sea. Fentafriddle is just a mile's walk to scenic Trebarwith Strand Beach. It is a renowned surfing spot. David is a super-keen surfer and although Emma claims not to be built for it, she and the children love the beach, bodyboarding, and wave jumping. David surfs in all weather and in the summer can be found catching waves in the late evenings after putting the children to bed. For his fortieth birthday, Emma gave him a longboard with the names of the family inscribed on it.

Emma and David met at Cambridge University, and they bonded over their shared love of Cornwall. Emma grew up in Oxfordshire, but her close friend at boarding school was Sarah Fortescue, whose parents used to host wonderful weekends away from school at Boconnoc (see page 33), and that's when she first fell in love with the county. Given David's passion for surfing, the couple, when they were in their twenties, would spend every weekend they could in Cornwall. It was a joyous getaway from their hectic jobs in the city. After they married and started a family, they wanted their three boys—George, Wilf, and Otis—to experience Cornwall too. Now the boys are obsessed with it. In fact, practically the first word that came out of Otis's mouth was "Fentafriddle."

The family divide their time between Cornwall and London and come to Fentafriddle as often as they can. The house is also used by Emma's and David's extensive families, so rarely a week passes without the house being occupied. The Deans love it in all seasons. "It's such a wonderful winter house," says Emma. With its log burner in the sitting room and AGA in the kitchen, "it is great to huddle down and watch the dramatic weather fronts out at sea." They enjoy winter walks down the valley to Backways Cove, finishing at the pub by the local beach. At Christmas they can manage to squeeze twenty people into the house (including babies sleeping in bathrooms and cupboards). The Christmas tree is the first thing you see when you open the front door, and every guest is charged with bringing a decoration for it—so the tree gets fuller every

**ABOVE:** The sitting room is full of fabulous fabrics. The David Seyfried chairs are covered in a fabric by Fermoie. The Arlo & Jacob sofa is covered in a bespoke fabric from de Le Cuona. The ottoman is covered in fabric from Rapture & Wright. The rug is from Birdie Fortescue.

**OPPOSITE:** The walls of the Games Room are painted Farrow & Ball Oval Room Blue. The boys are learning to play chess. David's mother is a Gujarati Indian, and this is her chessboard. The scalloped-edge sisal rug is from Tate and Darby. The blue leather chairs are vintage B&B Italia. The lamb above the fireplace is a print bought at the Affordable Art Fair in Battersea.

year. The turkey is cooked by David on a Big Green Egg BBQ whatever the weather. After Christmas, family moves out and friends move in for New Year celebrations. This involves early fireworks for the children who are then put to bed so that the adult party can begin, with much dancing and silly games.

On the day that the Deans moved into the house, Emma found a prettily framed four-leaf clover left behind for them in the kitchen. It was a present from the granddaughter of the previous owner who was actually born in the house (in an upstairs bathroom) in 2013. On the back of the frame was a note: "Hello! I am the Scott's youngest granddaughter. I was born here! Here is a four-leaf clover I found in a field in Fentafriddle that I thought you might like. Best wishes and Good Luck, Juno." This charming keepsake now hangs in the kitchen and when she passes it, Emma often reflects on how very lucky she is to be in such a magical place.

**ABOVE:** Emma bought the clock in the sitting room from Kempton Park Market for £100. "It's one of my favourite things in the house—and it works!"

**RIGHT:** Emma bought the piano from Facebook Marketplace for just £10, "but it cost many, many multiples of that to transport it down here from London." The bookshelves behind are painted Farrow & Ball Hague Blue. The piano stool fabric is from Rapture & Wright.

The kitchen table was made by the furniture maker Jack Leith—a friend of Emma's. The red chairs are by La Redoute. The ancient Cornish map is a replica from King's Court Galleries on Fulham Road in London.

**ABOVE:** All the baths in the house are vintage and originally came from Lanhydrock (a nearby historic house). Emma's bathroom is painted Farrow & Ball Lichen green. The painting of an estuary came from Sunbury Antiques Market in Kempton.

**RIGHT:** This window seat in Emma's bedroom looks out to sea. A Beata Heuman cushion sits below embroidered linen curtains on dormer rods.

**ABOVE:** Emma's own bed is from Ensemblier. Her interior designer, Isabelle Lomas, upholstered it in green velvet. The bedside tables are made from antique (mismatched) bedpan stands found on eBay. The lamps on them are from Tyson London. There is an OKA stool at the end of the bed. The reading lights are from Pooky, and the carpet was designed by Isabelle.

**ABOVE:** Fermoie drapery around the four-poster bed in the main guest bedroom. Curtains from Chelsea Textiles. Throws from Etsy. The cushions come from Caravane.

**OPPOSITE ABOVE:** Green iron beds in the boys' room were left behind by the previous owner, as they wouldn't fit through the door to get out of the room. The painting above was bought in the souk in Marrakesh. The bedside table is an old toy box from a neighbour. The cushions on the beds are by Beata Heuman. Emma designed the chequerboard-patterned floor, which was very complicated to paint and "almost caused the builders to lose the will to live."

**OPPOSITE BELOW LEFT:** This guest bedroom is known as the Mary Smith Room, after this dominating portrait. It was painted in 1785 by the Royal Academician James Northcote, who was a pupil of Joshua Reynolds. Mary was a relation of Emma's, and one of her daughters married the anti-slavery campaigner William Wilberforce.

**OPPOSITE BELOW RIGHT:** Lewis & Wood flyfishing wallpaper on the walls of the downstairs loo, which has an old Plymouth drop-flush lavatory

Carrs
CORNISH TEA
CORNISH COFFEE
Organic

**OPPOSITE:** The kitchen island came from Monkey and Bird and is topped with Verde Luana marble from stone importer MGLW in Battersea. Isabelle Lomas designed the free-standing red fridge. It is "absolutely inspired—completely fabulous," says Emma.

**RIGHT:** Emma found this painting of a smoking Cornish farmer on eBay. It cost £50. Emma restored the frame and painted it red and gold. It has become, she says, "the most precious piece of art I own because I love it so much."

**FAR RIGHT:** The portrait above the butler's sink is of Emma's mother as a child wearing a pink dress.

**BELOW:** A bespoke corner sofa with shelves underneath. A tilt-top table from Etsy with a little red lamp from OKA. The painting above the sofa is actually the lid of an old toy box that Emma found at Kempton Park Market.

# Great Trevarren
## *The prettiest house in Cornwall*

Gavin and Clare Green and their three daughters, Elsbeth, Alberta, and Dilys, had long dreamt of a home in Cornwall. Living in an end-of-terrace house ("with a postage-stamp-sized back garden") in Blackheath, South London, they found themselves longing for the peace and beauty of the county where they traditionally spent their summer holidays. Clare would idly browse the property pages and one day spotted a house just three miles outside Fowey, an area they knew well. It was an unusual house: not much bigger than their London home, but it came with five acres of land and seemed almost unbelievably pretty. The family took a trip to see it the first chance they had. "When the girls saw the house, their mouths literally fell open," says Gavin. "They were completely blown away." Not an unusual reaction, for Great Trevarren, a piece of perfectly symmetrical Queen Anne architecture, has often been called the prettiest house in Cornwall. In fact, the *Sunday Times* once went further and called it "Britain's Most Beautiful House."

Great Trevarren was built around 1705 of locally quarried Pentewan stone with granite dressings. Attached to the front south-facing façade are four full-height Ionic columns that extend into the eaves. Its panelled front door is topped by a pretty fanlight and sits under an elegant semicircular pediment. It is delightful in every way. "It is just so incredibly impressive and beautiful and romantic," says Gavin, "but when you enter you realise that it is only one room deep and not the grand mansion that the outside suggests. It's like a doll's house and very theatrical." Quite apt for Gavin, who, as co-founder of Charcoalblue theatre consultants, has been responsible for helping to design theatre spaces around the world over the last twenty years.

Not much is known about the house. For the past two centuries it has been a working farmhouse, but it certainly doesn't resemble the typical Cornish farmer's dwelling.

What little history the Greens do know comes from a letter that the great Cornish scholar, poet, and historian A. L. Rowse wrote to a previous owner in 1957, thanking her for a tour of the house. "I promised to let you

The classical façade of Great Trevarren, built c.1705

know something of its history," Rowse wrote. "Trevarren belonged to a junior branch of the great Courtenay family—probably those settled at St. Cadoc's in St. Veep's parish—who sold it in 1700 to John Thomas, Esquire, who built the house in Queen Anne's reign. It has always, or for a long time, been in the hands of gentry: hence the distinction of the house and its unspoiled state . . . It is a treasure of a place, so perfect and unspoiled." What is a mystery is why Thomas decided to build such a beautiful house, in such a grand style, but on such a miniature scale.

The house's bewildering beauty was not the only thing that astounded the Greens when they first arrived at Great Trevarren. There were also flamingos in the pond at the front of the house and penguins at the back door, along with a pair of sun bears. The then owner had built a private zoo for conservation and his own pleasure on the five-acre site, including all manner of special buildings for housing his collection of cheetahs, wolves, and snow leopards. It was an extraordinary setup, and in 2018, a clouded leopard escaped from the property and spent a week on the run before finally being caught in a fox trap. But the Greens were not put off and, indeed, remain charmed by some of the eccentric landscaping the zookeeper left behind, including a tea plantation, ancient tree ferns and banana trees, various tropical plants, and giant phormiums.

The Greens were captivated by the house (who wouldn't be?) and quickly made the move from London. As it was a similar size, they were largely able to fill the house with the contents of their Blackheath home. Gavin and Clare have always liked modern and mid-century furniture. They appreciate good craftsmanship, and various classic twentieth-century designs can be found throughout the house; for example, the iconic Ligne Roset Togo sofa in the living room that was designed in 1973 by Michel Ducaroy.

The Greens immediately felt at home. "On the day we moved in our neighbour turned up with a brace of pheasants, our decorator welcomed us with two lobsters, and we found a bag of apples by the front door," says Gavin. "Everyone we met was warm and friendly." The girls have embraced country living. They were invited to watch calves being born by the dairy farmer next door. Another neighbour has an owl box and called them over to see the owl man tag the owlets. Gavin has also thrown himself into Cornish life and has joined a Pilot Gig team in Fowey. These six-oar rowing boats, built of Cornish narrow-leaf elm, date back to the seventeenth century, when they were used as shore-based lifeboats that went to vessels in distress. Today they are used competitively for racing and even have a world championship. Gavin loves it. "It's a really community-focused activity and very sociable." Which makes the training in the dark on a freezing morning in February seem worthwhile. He

**ABOVE:** String system shelving in the kitchen—classic Swedish design

**LEFT:** The Greens are keen cooks—especially Elsbeth, who makes "awesome" sourdough bread in the Wolf oven in the kitchen. Peggy, the wire-haired dachshund, looks ready for her supper.

has also joined Fowey Sailing Club ("as an Improver—which I try not to take too badly") and dreams of one day owning a wooden-hulled Fowey River dinghy—an official class of small-keeled boat designed in the 1930s and a mainstay of the local club.

The garden and grounds take some work, but after cold, wet days the family like to return to the extremely cosy house and light a fire in the panelled drawing room. Leaving London was a monumental change for them all, but there is no doubting the pleasures of Cornwall and the joy of living in its prettiest house.

**ABOVE:** Olive sits on a blue sofa from Vitra. The Hector Bibendum light over the table is from Original BTC.

**OPPOSITE:** The kitchen dresser is from May and Co Interiors. On it are a pair of splatter plates from Arket, some brass candlesticks from Skandium, and a porcelain cow from Liberty.

NIGEL SLATER
NIGEL SLATER

**FAR LEFT:** A hidden door in the panelling reveals a cavernous drinks cupboard. Gavin is a keen cocktail maker and collects interesting Cornish artisan spirits like the Wrecking Coast Clotted Cream Gin, Organic Rose Gin by Tinkture, and a bottle of ready-mixed espresso martini from legendary Cornish chef Rick Stein.

**LEFT:** The red chair is an Eero Saarinen Womb Chair from the 1950s.

**BELOW:** The plasterwork pilasters in the Blue Room are painted into the original panelling. The copper wall lights are by Tom Dixon. The Steinmayer piano is played by Alberta and Elsbeth. The "Love" poster came from a shop on Columbia Road in London.

**OPPOSITE:** The snug, also known as the White Room, is painted in Au Lait by Farrow & Ball. The blue seats are from the Ligne Roset Togo modular collection, designed in 1973 by Michel Ducaroy. The cushions are by Eleanor Pritchard.

**ABOVE:** String bookshelves and a Vitra Polder sofa on the stair landing

**RIGHT:** The hall is painted in Strong White by Farrow & Ball with Ammonite on the panelling.

**OPPOSITE:** The mirrored pendant light hanging above the hall is by Tom Dixon and is called Melt. The coat and hat stand is from Skandium. The Greens are particularly fond of Scandinavian design.

GET LOST

The Squiggly Career
HASHTAG AUTHENTIC
THE KITCHEN STUDIO
STUART TURTON
VERONICA ROTH

**OPPOSITE:** Alberta's bedroom. Her favourite colour is purple, and the walls are painted Calluna by Farrow & Ball. The bed is from Feather & Black. The beanbag is by Donna Wilson for SCP. The Pigeon Light is by Thorsten van Elten.

**RIGHT:** The tiny bath, and its fittings, came from Waterworks. The bathroom is painted Strong White by Farrow & Ball, and the floor tiles come from Fired Earth. The top picture of a mermaid and a scallop shell is by Jo Oakley, a friend and artist now based in Falmouth.

**ABOVE:** Gavin Green and his two wire-haired dachshunds, Olive and Peggy

**LEFT:** Great Trevarren's early eighteenth-century sash windows are tall and elegant and dressed in granite.

# Ince Castle
## *A private peninsula*

Anthony Draper's first real-life glimpse of Ince Castle was from the air, and he was immediately captured by its remarkable and romantic situation. The castle sits in splendid isolation on its own private peninsula jutting out into the River Lynher—three miles from Saltash. It is practically an island, surrounded on three sides by water. In fact, up until the First World War, before the bridge and drive were built, almost everything needed to service the house had to be brought across the river by boat. Anthony flies helicopters and piloted himself to his first viewing of the house. He had spotted it on the internet during a search for a country house for him and his husband, Peter Gain, and their two children, Max and Tom. Initially, they had been looking in the commuter belt around London and were close to buying a property in Surrey, but when Anthony saw the advert for Ince, he was intrigued. Peter was sceptical. It was far, far beyond their search area, and the couple barely knew Cornwall. But Anthony decided it was worth seeing anyway and flew down from London with a friend, suspecting the journey might prove to be nothing more than a jolly day out. Its remoteness turned out to be one of its greatest charms, and he managed to persuade Peter to come and see it too. Peter was particularly captivated by its sense of history, and six years later the family is happily ensconced in the castle, which they have lovingly done up, and Cornwall feels very much like home.

Grade I–listed Ince Castle has quite a history. It is actually not a castle in the conventional sense, but rather an extraordinarily picturesque manor house built of brick, attached to which are four pyramid-roofed, battlemented towers, with walls four feet thick. It was built in 1642 at the start of the English Civil War by Henry Killigrew, the Royalist Member of Parliament for West Looe, and is possibly the oldest brick house in Cornwall. The upper floors of its towers are now slate-hung but cover the original chequer-patterned brick-work. Legend has it that Killigrew kept four wives at Ince, one in each tower, each unknown to the others. A rather unlikely story, as the castle, although impressive in design, is relatively modest in size and Killigrew, even if he had been so inclined, would have struggled to keep four spouses secret from one

A view of the house from the south gardens

**ABOVE:** Anthony and Ollie the spaniel outside the front of Ince

**OPPOSITE ABOVE:** The south façade of the Jacobean castle

**OPPOSITE BELOW:** The swimming pool, which has fabulous views across the Lynher River towards Antony—another of Cornwall's great houses (see page 16)

another. Ince was besieged and captured by Parliamentarian forces in 1646. It was subsequently owned by Edward Nosworthy, the mayor of Truro, and then by John Hobart, 1st Earl of Buckinghamshire, before being passed into the Pryn family in the eighteenth century. The Pryns, and their descendants, farmed it until the early twentieth century. The Earl of St. Germans bought it in 1918 and made considerable alterations before selling it, in 1922, to H. R. "Bobby" Somerset, whose yacht *Jolie Brise* was a multiple winner of the Fastnet Race and was kept in the boathouse at Ince Castle. In 1960, it was bought by Alan and Patricia Lennox-Boyd (the 1st Viscount and Viscountess Boyd of Merton). It suffered a devastating fire in 1988, apparently caused by a smouldering cigarette, and nearly every room was destroyed. It had to be almost completely rebuilt. The post-fire restoration was carried out by the neoclassical architect Anthony Jaggard, who installed, amongst other things, the cantilevered central staircase. It was then lived in by the 2nd Viscount and Viscountess Boyd until they sold it to Anthony and Peter in 2018.

The couple's first act upon moving in was to hire Ben Pentreath, the much-celebrated English country house architect and interior designer. Ben had lots of brilliant ideas about reconfiguring the house with a view to creating a more Jacobean feel to the place. But, ultimately, rather than undertake years of onerous planning applications and building work, the couple decided to commission a redecoration rather than a complete refurbishment. So, Ben and his assistant, Leo Kary, updated bathrooms, designed wardrobes, painted and wallpapered every room in the house, and sourced nearly all of the furniture, but left the bones of the building pretty much as they were.

The centre of the house, and of family life, is Squirrel Hall—so named after the carvings on the fire surround. This room has the best, and most generously sized, fireplace in the house. Peter likes to sit and read here, and Anthony likes to listen to music, and it is also where they often have drinks before dinner. A large pair of Tannoy Prestige speakers reveal Anthony's love of music. He used to work in music distribution and loves all styles of music, but particularly jazz (he plays the saxophone). Twelve-year-old Max much prefers rap. The fireback features a phoenix, which represents the house being brought back to life after the disastrous 1988 fire. Directly off this hall is the dining room, which is slightly small for an eleven-bedroom house. Ben Pentreath investigated moving a wall to create a bigger space, but it proved tricky in the Grade I listed house. In the end they left it as is, and by adding a trestle table at one end to make a T shape, it can seat eighteen.

Scattered throughout the house is art by South African painters, photographers, and sculptors. Both Anthony and Peter were born in Johannesburg.

They met at prep school and were childhood friends but didn't get together until after university. Coming from South Africa, the couple find English weather occasionally challenging; hence when picking their own bedroom at Ince, they chose one situated over the boiler room and consequently the warmest room in the house. It looks out across the river, towards Antony, another of Cornwall's great and historic houses (see page 17).

Ince Castle's gardens are breathtaking. Isabel and Julian Bannerman worked on them extensively and helped design the new boathouse on the southern shore of the peninsula. Built from green oak, it looks rather like an upturned ship. It has an ingenious first-floor balcony that can be raised and lowered like a drawbridge. From here the family can watch river life in all its glory, including black-tailed godwits foraging on the foreshore. These long-billed birds are far safer under Anthony and Peter's stewardship of the peninsula than they would have been in Henry Killigrew's day. For in the seventeenth century, they were much prized as a delicacy and were hunted mercilessly. Today, Ince Castle boasts a Belgian chef called Phillipe who specialises in vegetarian food, and life is altogether more civilised.

**ABOVE:** Squirrel Hall, as it is known because of the motifs over the fireplace. The corduroy footstool was designed by Ben Pentreath. The sofa is covered in a William Morris print with a modern colourway.

**OPPOSITE:** Max and Ollie on the cantilevered staircase in the main hall

**ABOVE:** The South Garden room, a very light room that the family use for drinks in the summer. The Scrolling Fern Silhouette wallpaper is by Soane. The photograph of the Karoo is by South African artist David Goldblatt.

**LEFT:** In the TV room, a Greek key motif runs around the walls beneath the cornicing. The large charcoal drawing is by the celebrated South African artist William Kentridge. Leo Kary (who works for Ben Pentreath) designed the coffee table.

**OPPOSITE:** Ollie the spaniel (who belongs to Phillipe the chef) relaxing on the linoleum floor in the kitchen. The wallpaper is Willow Boughs by Morris & Co. The fabric of the curtains and on the chairs is Magnolia by GP & J Baker.

PAUL
RAWLEN
ROBUCHON
SWEET

**ABOVE:** The antique wallpaper in the downstairs loo dates to the eighteenth century and is original to the house. The framed collection of butterflies and moths is a popular English country house motif.

**RIGHT:** The burnt-orange colour of the dining room is The Long Room from Paint & Paper Library. The tablecloth is from Rebecca Udall and the Oriente Italiano plates are from Richard Ginori. The table is dressed with blue hydrangeas.

**ABOVE:** The bathroom en suite to the Chinese bedroom—with direct access into the garden

**RIGHT:** The Chinese bedroom on the ground floor has original eighteenth-century hand-painted wallpaper.

**LEFT:** The first-floor study, which leads into the primary bedroom

**OPPOSITE ABOVE:** The walls of the drawing room are hung with an oyster-coloured linen. The sofa in the foreground came from Hawker Antiques and is covered in a green silk. The matching pair of sofas are from Howard & Sons. The eighteenth-century portrait above the fire was bought at Christie's.

**OPPOSITE BELOW:** The family use the drawing room for game playing and music practice as well as formal entertaining. The neoclassical sofa was covered by Ben Pentreath in a bottle-green silk.

**ABOVE:** A cream-coloured AGA in the kitchen at Ince. The burnt orange walls reflect the collection of copper pans.

**OPPOSITE:** The ultimate luxury—a dedicated flower room, used for arranging the great bounty from the cutting gardens

# Marratons
## *Hawker's house*

The Reverend Robert Stephen Hawker, known to his parishioners as Parson Hawker, was arguably the most famous Cornishman of the Victorian era. He was both a priest and a poet and wrote Cornwall's unofficial national anthem—"Trelawny"—which starts with the famous stanza "A good sword and a trusty hand! A merry heart and true! King James's men shall understand what Cornish lads can do!" He was also a renowned eccentric—he dressed as a mermaid, excommunicated his cat, became addicted to morphine, and was once accused of hanging a mouse. But beyond all this, he was most well-known for his insistence on the compassionate burial of shipwrecked souls who washed up on the shores of his coastal parish of Morwenstow.

The north Cornish coastline is famous for its rugged and dramatic beauty, but along with being an inspiration to artists and writers alike, it was, and to some extent remains, a place of great danger. Its seabed is littered with the wrecks of thousands of ships. It was soon after he arrived as vicar of Morwenstow in 1842 that Parson Hawker first experienced a shipwreck—of a Scottish brig called the *Caledonia*. He vividly described it in an article in a magazine published by Charles Dickens:

> About daybreak I was aroused by a knock at my bedroom-door; it was followed by the agitated voice of a boy, "There are dead men on vicarage rocks!" In a moment I was up, and in my dressing-gown and slippers rushed out. I ran a quarter of a mile, to the cliffs, and down a frightful descent of three hundred feet to the beach. It was indeed a scene to be looked on only once in a human life. On a ridge of rock, stood a man with two dead sailors at his feet, whom he had just drawn out of the water stiff and stark. The bay was tossing and seething with a tangled mass of rigging, sails, and broken fragments of a ship and anon there came up out of the water, as though stretched out with life, a human hand and arm. It was the corpse of another sailor drifting out to sea.

Before Hawker, it was common practice for the carcasses of shipwrecked men to be cast into a pit, dug just above the high-water mark, without inquest or religious rite. The parson found this too barbaric to contemplate and carried

The exterior of Marratons. The whole house is trimmed in Farrow & Ball's St Giles Blue.

the corpses of the men up the cliffs himself, insisted on a coroner's inquest, conducted funeral services, and buried the men in the churchyard of St. Morwenna (named after a local saint). He continued to do this, with all too terrible frequency, over the forty years of his residence as parson.

On his arrival in the parish, Hawker set about building himself a glebe house. During its two-year construction he lived in a house called Marratons, half a mile away. Little is known about the early history of Marratons, and there is no record of it in the National Archives. Old maps show the property as "Marratons Cottage," and in the eighteenth century it was a farm of around thirty acres. The "nursery end" is plainly much older than the main part of the house. It is built of stone, with cob on the upper parts. The roof was probably originally of thatch. Its present owner is Alice Gates, co-founder of Barneby Gates, the wallpaper and fabric studio.

Marratons was bought by Alice's grandfather Charles Barrington shortly before the start of World War II. According to Alice, Charles was something of a rake who "fled Liverpool in a cloud of shame owing a lot of money." Rich relations helped him buy Marratons in the hope that he couldn't get into too much trouble in remote North Cornwall. It seemed to work, and Charles went on to live a happy life there, providing a bucolic childhood for Alice's mother, Geraldine, and her two brothers (both of whom played cricket for Cornwall). When Alice inherited the house in 2021, it had been largely untouched since her grandparents had first remodelled it in 1939. With her keen designer's eye, she set to work updating it and filling it with her beautiful papers and fabrics.

Alice studied painting in Florence before doing an MA in fine art at City and Guilds in London. She made her living as an artist before teaming up with her childhood friend Vanessa Barneby (then Living editor at *Vogue*) to create their eponymous firm. Their wallpapers, which are globally admired, are "steeped in English tradition and heritage but with a modern twist." Marratons is a perfect showcase for their brilliant work, but more importantly, it is a beautiful home to Alice, her husband, Harry, and their three children, who love it every bit as much as Alice did when she was a child.

The house sits right on the border between Devon and Cornwall. Alice's nearest friend lives on the other side of the valley, which is actually in Devon. But there is no blurring of the line, and Alice is proud of her Cornish heritage and definitely eats her clotted cream teas the Cornish way (putting jam on the scone first and then cream on top). "Unlike the savages in Devon who put jam on top of the cream," she says, "I couldn't bring myself to eat a scone like that!" Beautiful walks abound in every direction. Stanbury Beach, where Alice would surf as a child, is half a mile away. The Gateses like to load up rucksacks

**ABOVE LEFT:** The Church of St. Morwenna in Morwenstow

**ABOVE RIGHT:** Alice on the steps of Marratons

to spend the day there, taking cricket bats, surfboards, and a BBQ. They set up camp on a particular flat rock, which they always commandeer, and know the best rock pools to forage in. "The beach and its traditions are unchanged since my mother's day. We cook sausages and burgers, and occasionally lobsters. We carry down beer and bottles of wine. It is always a feast. Just taking a ham sandwich would be a bit depressing. The dogs love the surf and go a bit nuts before, invariably, drinking from a rock pool and then being sick when they get back to the house."

The family also often wander up to Morwenstow church, which holds a special place in their hearts. Alice and Harry were married there, and Alice's grandparents and mother are buried there. Their resting place is a large tabletop tomb not far from a replica of the figurehead from the *Caledonia*, which Parson Hawker had erected to the memory of its captain and crew.

**ABOVE:** The picture above the fireplace is a late eighteenth-century portrait of "the Barrington Boys"—ancestors of Alice's. They look seriously mischievous. The wall colour is Edward Bulmer's Lilac Pink. The armchair on the right is covered in Scallop Shell by Barneby Gates. The sofa was inherited, and Alice reupholstered it in pink houndstooth. The yellow lacquered tray on the ottoman is from Addison Ross.

**RIGHT:** The dining area of the open-plan ground floor. The table and chairs were always in the house. The tablecloth is from LNH Edit (in Dublin). The Plymouth Gin Glug Jug was a present from Alice's business partner, Vanessa. The cabinetry is painted Little Greene Royal Navy. There are lots of prints by Josephine Trotter.

**OPPOSITE ABOVE AND ABOVE LEFT:** Alice's bed was made by a local carpenter. The bedcover comes from Birdie Fortescue. The painting on the far wall (opposite above) is by Alice herself, of her friend Suzie's house across the valley. The room is covered in Strawberry Trellis wallpaper by Barneby Gates.

**OPPOSITE BELOW:** The tongue-and-groove panelling around the bath is painted in Blazer by Farrow & Ball. The slate ends are from Delabole quarry. The Barneby Gates wallpaper is Lattice Cane. The rug is from Tate and Darby, and the giant shell is not from Cornwall but from the Cayman Islands!

**ABOVE RIGHT:** This twin bedroom is called the Shell Room, after the headboards that are covered in red Scallop Shell fabric by Barneby Gates. The bedcover is from SARAH.K, the owl cushions are from Etsy, and the lampshade is from Birdie Fortescue. The crab mug is from John Lewis & Partners.

**ABOVE:** The side table in the hall was inherited. On it sit Pooky lamp bases with lampshades from Loving String. The Barneby Gates wallpaper is Diamond Trellis.

**RIGHT:** The TV room is also known as the Green Room because of its vibrant Emerald Green paint by Farrow & Ball. The painting of chrysanthemums is by Janet Kidd. The coronation cups on the dado were collected by Alice's mother. The corner sofa is from Sofas & Stuff, and the stripy cushions are by Andrew Martin.

**ABOVE:** One of the smartest greenhouses this author has seen is attached to the kitchen and acts as a flower room.

**OPPOSITE:** The bookshelves in the study are painted in Farrow & Ball's Railings. They contain a fabulous collection of novels by early twentieth-century writer E. Phillips Oppenheim.

BYRON
NAPOLEON
PIRACY
MICHAEL ARLEN
THE TITLED NOBILITY OF EUROPE
THE AGE OF NAPOLEON

SMEG

Alice prefers an Everhot to an AGA—"easy to control, cheaper to run." A mirrored wall above it makes the room appear far bigger. A fluted butler's sink lets one do the washing up whilst looking onto the rear garden.

# Pirate's Manor
## *The Killigrews' hideout*

Rosemullion Head has always been a strategically important spot. Situated three miles south of Falmouth (which is the world's third-largest natural harbour), it guards the entrance to the Helford River. Just outside the headland's tiny village of Mawnan is a Grade II listed manor house. It is known as Pirate's Manor, to reflect its extraordinary history.

Pirate's Manor, along with the entire headland, was acquired by the infamous Killigrew family in the late 1500s. This great seafaring clan had been a dominant force in Cornish society for centuries and played a significant role in shaping Falmouth's maritime history, with various family members holding high office. But the family also has a notorious reputation for smuggling and piracy. The critical position of the manor at the mouth of the Helford and the wooded creeks and inlets of the river's estuary provided perfect cover for all manner of maritime skulduggery. Sir John Killigrew was a wily politician and businessman but often found himself on the wrong side of the law. Both he and his son spent time locked in the Tower of London for their crimes, which was somewhat ironic, considering Sir John also served on a commission for piracy in Cornwall. Killigrew wives had as fearsome a reputation as their husbands. Sir John's wife, Mary Wolverston, was widely held to be involved in all manner of horrifying maritime deeds. She even stood trial for seizing a Spanish ship that had taken shelter in Falmouth and murdering its crew while the captain and first mate were being entertained by her husband. Two of her servants were found guilty and executed, but she received a pardon at the eleventh hour from Queen Elizabeth. Half a century later, Sir John's granddaughter-in-law Jane Killigrew was similarly suspected of launching murderous raids on innocent merchantmen anchored in Falmouth Bay and was also accused of "flagrant prostitution." They were certainly a characterful bunch. But families such as the Killigrews, corrupt as they might have been, continued to thrive in their lawlessness, as the authorities thought it best to keep them on their side, given England's susceptibility to seaborne invasion.

Looking from the stables towards the bay windows of the Victorian wing of the house

The clock tower, which also doubles as a dovecote, stands in the stable yard next to the house.

Pirate's Manor sits slightly inland, above the mouth of the Helford, giving it protection from battering storms. The present house is an eighteenth-century reconstruction of the much larger manor house that would have stood here before, one whose origins dated back to the thirteenth century. It was further developed by the Victorians and is now an L-shaped house surrounded by walled gardens. A charming clock tower and dovecote stand in the stable yard next to the house. The house itself is built from sandy-coloured killas stone and it is approached by an enchanting avenue lined with yew trees.

It is home to Suzy Hoodless, her husband, Erskine Berry, and their three children, Misty, Myla, and Arki. Suzy is one of Britain's leading interior designers and part of the founding team of *Wallpaper** magazine. Her interior style has been described as a kind of alchemy: a creative mix of styles and eras with a bold approach to colour and a touch of the unexpected. She maintains, with all her projects, that it is important to be inspired by the architecture of the building. The family bought the house four years ago. They like this area, as they feel that the South Coast is where people actually live, rather than the North Coast, which is dominated by holidaymakers.

On one's arrival at the house, a pillared portico leads into a hallway that is flagged with slate and bordered by reclaimed church pews. This in turn leads to a huge forty-foot-long open-plan kitchen and dining room with French doors leading onto a slate terrace and the sprawling lawns of the garden beyond. There is a large navy-blue AGA range in an alcove stuffed with cookbooks, lots of them concerning seafood and written by some of the many great chefs Cornwall has produced. The whole family loves to cook. Mussels are a particular favourite, and the children "bake furiously," says Suzy. There is a nautical air to the room, with its wooden beams like a ship's rafters and a writing desk at the far end of the room, which has an antique captain's chair in front of it. Beyond the kitchen, a sumptuous drawing room with floor-to-ceiling sash windows gives a sense of the historic manorial status of the house. It is a room made comfortable by Suzy with huge sofas and an ottoman perfectly suited for puzzling, Monopoly, and cards. Hanging on the walls is a collection of glass-encased model sailing ships that summon up the house's piratical past. Continuing on into the Victorian wing of the house, there is a handsome library with wood-panelled walls and built-in bookcases. Upstairs are five blissful bedrooms, some with beautiful bay windows, and all charming, including a pleasingly old-fashioned children's bedroom adorned with vintage wallpaper.

The garden at Pirate's Manor is full of trees and shrubs that thrive in this part of the world's subtropical climate, including a dahlia brought back from the Himalayas by a previous owner. There are butterflies fluttering in the wisteria on the day we visit. Because of its proximity to the sea, it never actually freezes here. It does rain a lot, like everywhere in England, but that doesn't put off the Berry family from going to the beach, and they sail and swim in all weather. There are lots of fantastic beaches nearby. A footpath from the house leads down to Prisk Cove, and another, from St. Mawnan Church, goes down to the beaches on the north shore of the Helford River. The tranquil waters of the estuary are perfect for paddleboarding. Sometimes, the family paddle across the passage to the Shipwrights pub. They try to stay dry on the way across, but someone inevitably falls in on the way back. "But at least there's no drink driving involved," says Erskine. The family also like to kayak up the river, seeking out the caves and hideaways once used by the Killigrew family, on modern-day piratical adventures of their own.

The L-shaped eighteenth-century Pirate's Manor

**ABOVE:** The kitchen desk belonged to Suzy's grandfather. In front of it is an antique ship captain's chair. A vintage map of Cornwall hangs above.

**RIGHT:** Around the farmhouse kitchen table is a miscellany of stick-back Windsor chairs—some with a wheel motif—from Lay's Auctioneers in Penzance.

**ABOVE:** The drawing room at Pirate's Manor. The ottoman was commissioned by Suzy from Sedilia, as was the sofa, which was made to Suzy's own design and is covered in a Claremont fabric.

**ABOVE:** The stripy sofa in the drawing room is 1950s Danish and came already covered from the dealer. The cushions, including one with crab and seahorse motifs, were bought in Venice. "It's always nice to bring something back from travelling abroad," says Suzy. The wall hanging came from Robert Kime.

DBC PIERRE
CATASTROPHE
KHRUSHCHEV
PIRATES

**ABOVE:** Wood-panelled walls and built-in bookcases in the library

**OPPOSITE:** Behind the mid-century Danish desk is a green covered Vitra Eames chair. The curtains are made with a fabric from Pierre Frey.

**ABOVE:** The main guest bedroom has curtains and cushions made with Robert Kime's "Indian Pear." The quilt was made by Pat Giddens in a Marvic Textiles Misa Moire Stripe.

**LEFT:** A pleasingly old-fashioned children's bedroom adorned with vintage wallpaper that came with the house. There are Babar the Elephant prints hanging above the bed.

**ABOVE:** The chair in the yellow bedroom is covered in a fabric from Pierre Frey.

**RIGHT:** The yellow bedroom. The painted wardrobe beyond is eighteenth-century Austrian.

# Trebenny
## *Betjeman country*

St. Enodoc in Trebetherick is a tiny twelfth-century church nestled amongst the sand dunes of Daymer Bay. It sits at the foot of Brae Hill and has a bent spire like a wonky witch's hat. For several centuries it was virtually buried by the wind-driven sand from the dunes that surround it and was known locally as "Sinking Neddy." In the early nineteenth century, it was so deeply sunk that once a year the local vicar had to be lowered on a rope through a hole in the roof in order to conduct a service and maintain its consecration. Finally, in 1864, it was dug out and the dunes were stabilised. Today it stands as a much-loved parish church, surrounded by the rolling fairways and greens of St. Enodoc Golf Club. Nowadays, the church is best known for its indelible links to the poet laureate Sir John Betjeman—one of Cornwall's most famous sons. Or "adopted son," one should say, as Betjeman's family weren't Cornish at all, just long-term holidaymakers on the north Cornish coast. But Sir John loved the county deeply and lived there for much of his life, and a considerable volume of his work was a celebration of the "Delectable Duchy."

Betjeman knew the church well as a child, and, indeed, one of the first poems he ever wrote, aged eight, was "The St. Enodock Ghost." Both his parents are buried there, as is the poet himself, under a slab of Delabole slate—his name and dates carved in Gothic letters surrounded by pretty engravings of honeybees, oak leaves, and barleycorns.

When Betjeman, as a small boy, first came to Trebetherick, there was only one motorcar in the parish, the roads were dirt tracks, and everyone in the village used oil lamps and candles. Trebetherick of today is somewhat different, with its crowds of holidaymakers, Range Rover–clogged roads, and a chic delicatessen. Yet much remains the same: the springy thyme-scented turf, the circling seagulls, the bramble hedges thick with sloes and blackberries, and families busying themselves rock-pooling, beach-cricketing, and hunting for tiny pink cowrie shells on Greenaway Beach. The simple pleasures of Trebetherick are much as Betjeman knew them, and it's still a land of picnics, bridge parties,

The dining terrace of Trebenny with its views over Brae Hill, St. Enodoc golf course, and Daymer Bay—Betjeman country and drinks at the golf club. Trebenny, set just back from the golf course, is a house Betjeman would have known. It was built in the 1930s as a beach house and is next to asparagus fields that once belonged to the Betjeman family. It is now the home of Guy and Ruth East, who bought it twenty-five years ago and commissioned a brilliant young architect called Steve Heaver to remodel and extend it. Heaver designed the entrance to the house to mimic the lychgate of St. Enodoc Church—which is a pretty roofed structure with a slate stand used by pallbearers to rest their coffins whilst they wait for funeral services to begin. Inside the house, the rooms on the ground floor flow seamlessly into one another, and the curved walls reference the rolling landscape in which the house sits. Huge windows fill the house with soft Cornish light and frame the breathtaking views of field and sea, Brae Hill, and the crooked steeple of St. Enodoc poking up from the golf course. The roof is made of slate tiles hung in diminishing courses in the traditional manner.

Ruth, a television and film producer who worked for the BBC for many years, is a keen art collector. She has filled the house with paintings and sculptures, often by Cornish artists, many associated with the St. Ives School—like Breon O'Casey and Wilhelmina Barns-Graham. She is also, of course, a Betjeman fan, and the house abounds with his books and other paraphernalia, including a wonderful print, in the downstairs loo, of his funeral procession. It is by Trebetherick-based artist Joan Crockett and shows the train of mourners huddled under umbrellas as they crossed the golf course on foot on their way to St. Enodoc.

Ruth has eight grandchildren who all spend parts of their summer holidays with her at Trebenny. They play golf and tennis, water-ski in the Camel Estuary, collect shells on the beach, and swim in the pool that the Easts had built on the site of an old tortoise-racing track (!) at the bottom of the garden. They sound like summers every bit as blissful as the ones Betjeman knew and which he immortalised in his poem "Trebetherick." It ends with a prayer that his own children might know the same happy days that he spent as a child on this most blessed part of the Cornish coast.

Enodoc is not the only saint connected to this part of the world. It was also the one-time home of Petroc—the unofficial patron saint of Cornwall. He was by all accounts a gentle man known for his kindness to animals and was celebrated for his many miracles, which included raising the dead, curing the sick, and taming savage monsters. He arrived in Cornwall in the fifth century after crossing the sea from Ireland in a tiny coracle boat. Wind and tides drove him into the mouth of the Camel Estuary, and the first place he set foot was Trebetherick. What a splendid place to wash up.

The kitchen is dominated by a very chic white AGA that Ruth turns off in the summer. The shelves house a collection of jugs and a print of St. Enodoc Church.

The dining room looks out over Brae Hill. You can see the wonky steeple of St. Enodoc Church peeking up over the gorse in the distance. The table was made in Devon, and the chairs come from The Conran Shop. The striped window seats were made of a French material from Saint-Tropez used for making deck chairs. Ruth bought the woven baskets in South Africa.

The coffee table in the sitting room is plate glass covering a collection of Rupert Spira celadon-blue dishes, each bearing a poetic phrase. The picture above the fire is by Scottish artist John Boyd. The rug is from Sinclair Till. Above the sofa on the right is a Howard Hodgkin painting titled *Ice Cream*.

**ABOVE:** The bespoke dresser in the dining room is made from driftwood by Edward Teasdale. The blue abstract painting above is by Wilhelmina Barns-Graham, who lived and worked in St. Ives.

**OPPOSITE:** The skyscape painting above the curved fireplace in the dining room is by British painter Tai-Shan Schierenberg. On the shelf to the right is a collection of shell figures made during lockdown by Ruth's daughter-in-law Sophie Pakenham.

**ABOVE RIGHT:** A corner of the sitting room. The hanging fish in the background are by Jilly Sutton, as is the carved wing on the pink wall beyond.

**TOP:** A carved wooden bust by Jilly Sutton in the dusky-pink kitchen

**ABOVE:** A Hamish Mackie puffin stands next to a collection of Betjeman books and a framed letter from the poet laureate himself.

**ABOVE RIGHT:** Guy East's collection of Staffordshire figures on an antique sideboard in the hall

**ABOVE:** The main guest bedroom. "On a stormy night it's a wonderful room to be in," says Ruth. The paintings on either side of the window are by Pamela Bianco. The chest of drawers came from Sotheby's—"It's probably a bit grand for Cornwall," says Ruth, "but I like painted furniture."

**RIGHT:** Ruth's bedroom, which has spectacular views over Daymer Bay. The headboard and valance are covered in a fabric by Fermoie. Over the bed are Hermione Owen drawings of Ruth's three children, Kate, Tom, and Edward.

**LEFT:** Three generations at play in the dining room

**BELOW:** Twelfth-century St. Enodoc Church, which overlooks the mouth of the Camel Estuary

**OPPOSITE:** Trebenny from the pool. The curved fence, made of old railway sleepers, reflects the shape of Brae Hill.

# Prideaux Place
## *An Elizabethan manor*

Prideaux Place is a Grade I listed Elizabethan manor house that overlooks Padstow, a natural harbour close to the mouth of the Camel Estuary. It is remarkable on a number of levels, not least that it is still lived in by the family who built it, nearly five hundred years ago. "I may be biased but I personally think that this is the loveliest place on earth." So speaks Peter Prideaux-Brune, the current patriarch. The Prideauxs are an ancient family who predate the Norman Conquest and have well over a thousand-year history in Cornwall. They were originally based at Prideaux Castle at Luxulyan, but Nicholas Prideaux, a prosperous lawyer, fell in love with, and bought, the manor of Padstow in 1539. His great-nephew, also called Nicholas, inherited the manor in 1582 and built the current house. It is a substantial and imposing house built in a classic Elizabethan E-plan, which some maintain was an homage to the reigning monarch herself. Its great hall and battlemented parapets give it the air of a castle. When Daniel Defoe passed through Padstow on his great tour of Britain in 1724, he described it thus: "a very ancient seat of a family of the name of Prideaux, who in Queen Elizabeth's time, built a very noble seat there, which remains to this day, tho' time makes the architect of it a little out of fashion." Defoe presumably would have approved of the remodelling of the southern front, that took place a century later, in an outstandingly attractive Strawberry Hill Gothic style. The house as it stands today is a wonderful mixture of neogothic, Georgian, and Elizabethan architecture, and its interiors are full of exquisite panelling, woodcarving, plasterwork, and furniture.

Prideaux Place is currently home to the fourteenth, fifteenth, and sixteenth consecutive generations of the Prideaux family: Peter and Elisabeth Prideaux-Brune; Peter's son and daughter-in-law, Nick and Martha; and their three daughters, Lila, Nell, and Kara. Not to mention three dogs: a flat-coated retriever called Tarka and two Labradors, Little and Norty, and three cats: Buddha, Bamboo, and Splodge. When one adds the herd of fallow deer in the ancient deer park that the house overlooks, it makes quite a menagerie.

The south façade of the house. This wing was built in a Strawberry Hill Gothic style named after Horace Walpole's house in Twickenham that originated this revival look in the mid-eighteenth century.

The deer park is thought to be one of the oldest in the country and has been dated back to its enclosure by the Romans in 435 AD. Legend has it that if the deer die out, so does the Prideaux family. Not wishing to test this alarming prediction, King George V sent a virile young buck from his herd at Windsor in 1927 when the bloodline was dwindling. Unfortunately, the animal did not get the chance to be of service, as the morning after his arrival a gamekeeper accidentally shot it. Luckily, the herd survived regardless, and despite numbers dropping to as few as six in the immediate aftermath of World War II, it now numbers more than one hundred, so the Prideaux family looks set to go for many more generations.

Deer aside, it is impressive that the family has survived so long, especially as they are, as Peter puts it, "politically inept." The Prideauxs backed the Parliamentarians during the English Civil War, and Edmund Prideaux managed to secure a pardon after the Restoration only by marrying off his sister to one of Charles II's key advisors. The Prideauxs' "knack for judicious marriages" continued down the years. At the end of the eighteenth century, Charles Prideaux married a great heiress who was the last of her line and added her name to his to become Prideaux-Brune. To celebrate his marriage (and new wealth), Charles built the drawing room wing in Horace Walpole's Strawberry Hill Gothic style.

Peter Prideaux-Brune was actually born in the house—in the Great Chamber, or the Susanna room, as it is sometimes called because of its intricately plastered ceiling depicting the biblical story of Susanna and the Elders. For centuries, this masterpiece was hidden away above a second ceiling that was hung below it when the room was divided into two. In the twentieth century the room was used as the nursery, and it was Peter himself who discovered the hidden ceiling whilst crawling around in the loft space as a young boy. "I found this entrance into the ceiling—a damp course—I crawled along and saw this amazing ceiling and told Father." It is now the centrepiece of tours around the house.

Nick and Martha Prideaux-Brune run the day-to-day operations of the house, which is open to the public during the week from April to October. They met through the theatre in London when they were both actors. The couple lived in London after marrying, but when their eldest girl, Lila, turned seven they decided to move full-time to Cornwall. Today they work at developing the estate, bringing events, dance shows, and theatre productions to the house. They are involved in restoring farmhouses and derelict buildings on the wider estate. Their current passion project is the restoration of the Prideaux Walled Garden. They have created a fantastic shop and café within the garden, which is gaining interest for their work with sustainable gardening practices and soil health.

The ancient deer park, which dates back to its enclosure by the Romans in 435 AD

Three generations living together in a house that is often filled with tourists is not without challenges. The house needs constant work, and some parts of it are completely unmodernised. One wing, for example, was last used by the US Army during World War II, when it took over the house. The soldiers left behind a certain amount of graffiti that can still be seen today, including a tribute to one Private First Class "Farty" Harper, who occupied one of the bedrooms.

Lila, albeit with some trepidation, looks forward to taking the house on when her time comes. She currently lives at the top of the North Tower, in a bedroom that used to be Nick's as a boy. It is dominated by a huge quatrefoil window that Nick remembers having sneaky cigarettes out of when he was a teenager. Lila, in a more civilised manner, uses it as a reading nook. As we leave, Lila and her sisters are being corralled by their mother to get ready for an evening trip to the beach. There is the usual chaotic scramble to find wet suits and picnic gear. Martha points out that the Prideaux-Brune family motto is "Toujours Pret"—always ready. "It really couldn't be more inappropriate," she says as they head down to the estuary.

The drawing room is painted in "Aubusson Yellow." The rug is a copy of an Aubusson made to the exact proportions of the room. The curtains are made from eau de Nil–coloured silk.

**ABOVE:** The Gothic theme continues into the bathroom, with Gothic arches in the bath surround and the same quatrefoil motif on the curtains as in the bedroom.

**RIGHT:** Known as the South Room because it sits above the south-facing lawn. The fabric on the headboard, valance, and trim on the curtains is based on a Gothic theme that reflects the giant quatrefoil window above the library.

**ABOVE:** A portrait of Henry Prideaux-Brune by Andrew Festing. The picture features Peter's teddy bear—known as "Me Too" after his insistence on being included in everything.

**OPPOSITE:** The huge Gothic arched window of the library overlooking the south lawn. Its stained-glass panels represent, in heraldic form, the history of the many heiresses the Prideauxs have married.

**ABOVE RIGHT:** The Grenville Drawing Room is named after the English Civil War hero Sir Richard Grenville, as the entire contents of the room, including the panelling, came from Stowe House (Grenville's mansion in Cornwall that was dismantled in the 1730s). The room is painted "Cornish green."

The Hall with its impressive cantilevered staircase. The floor was painted by a set designer during the filming here of Trevor Nunn's *Twelfth Night*, and the family liked it so much they kept it. Between the two hall tables is one of the oldest pieces of furniture in the house—a sixteenth-century chest inlaid with mother-of-pearl. It was salvaged from an armada ship that foundered in the Camel Estuary in 1588.

The dining room houses a mixture of Elizabethan and Georgian panelling. It includes a striking carving of Queen Elizabeth I standing on a pig, representing her stamping out vice. The table is laid with the family's crested Chamberlain Worcester dinner service.

**ABOVE:** The stairs on the right lead up to the library, and on the left to the North Tower and Lila's bedroom.

**OPPOSITE:** Kara, the youngest Prideaux-Brune, on a rocking horse below the "hidden ceiling" of the Great Chamber. The magnificent plasterwork was created in the sixteenth century by the Abbott family of Frithelstock. Kara's dog Tarka looks on.

TOUJOURS

**ABOVE:** Lila's bedroom, also known as the North Tower, includes the giant quatrefoil window that sits above the library. She uses it as an eyrie and a spot to read.

**RIGHT:** The North Tower, containing the library and a bedroom above, with its iconic quatrefoil window. The quatrefoil motif is repeated in decoration throughout the house.

**OPPOSITE:** Nick and Martha Prideaux-Brune with their daughters, Lila, Nell, and Kara. The girls are the sixteenth generation of Prideauxs to live at the house.

# Restormel Manor
## *Fit for a prince*

On the 17th of March, 1337, Edward III made his six-year-old son (also called Edward) the first Duke of Cornwall. Young Edward grew up to be known as "the Black Prince," hero of the Battle of Crécy and regarded by his English contemporaries as a model of chivalry and one of the greatest knights of his age. The Duchy of Cornwall that he was granted came with numerous manors and estates, not least of which was Restormel—one of the most remarkable castles in Britain.

Restormel was originally built shortly after the Norman Conquest, nearly one thousand years ago, as a motte and bailey castle. It was then converted into a perfectly circular "shell keep" with eight-foot-thick stone walls a century or so later. The architectural historian Pevsner calls it "by far the most perfect example of military architecture in Cornwall," but it was also built for luxurious living, with tranquil views across the Fowey Valley. Although a ruin today, its remains point to its past grandeur, with giant fireplaces, high windows, and an opulent great hall that mark it as much a palace as a fortified castle.

The Duchy was decreed by charter to be held by future eldest sons of kings of England in perpetuity. Cut to 2025 and the current, and 25th, duke is His Royal Highness William, Prince of Wales. His Cornish residence is not the magnificent Restormel Castle sitting proudly on its hill, but a rather more modest manor house, a few hundred yards below it, on the banks of the River Fowey.

Restormel Manor was originally a sixteenth-century farmhouse, remodelled in the eighteenth century as a Strawberry Hill Gothic–style manor house. It is built of slatestone rubble, rendered with granite dressings, and is most notable for its three-story, slate-hung, embattled porch, which is arguably a nod to the castle in whose shadow it sits.

It was the 24th duke (now His Majesty King Charles III) who decided to take the manor house back in hand after many years of tenancy. The Duchy decided to reconfigure the house into three separate rental units to be made available as short-term holiday lets, but it could also be used as a whole.

The wildflower meadow in front of the manor house

Furthermore, it was to become the official residence for the Duke of Cornwall when he was visiting the county. Annabel Elliot, the internationally renowned interior designer, was drafted in to help with the project. "It was quite a challenging brief!" she says. "My main worry was how could we manage to achieve the reconfiguration without in any way ruining the magic of Restormel. I wanted to keep the feeling of a wonderful old country house, which had evolved through the ages, but also had to comply with all sorts of rules and regulations for letting on the open market." Annabel worked closely with James Scott, who was in charge of building projects at the Duchy. The biggest undertaking was to create a large new kitchen at the back of the house, which would be the main one for the entire manor when the house was being used as a whole. Eventually, they created three different spaces: the central block known as the Manor (which sleeps eight), the Dairy House wing (which sleeps six), and a further wing called Trinity (which sleeps four). Each with its own entrance and kitchen, so as not to impact the others. Yet for big house parties, the doors between them can be opened up and the manor house used as a whole.

Restormel Manor is flooded with natural light thanks to its large Georgian sash windows (with the ones on the first floor shaped into attractive "Gothick" arches). When it came to decorating the house, Annabel embraced this and used mostly light colours—off-whites, pale blues and greens. Similarly, with the fabric for the curtains she used mostly natural linens, ticking, and, in some rooms, vintage linen sheets. Wherever she could, Annabel bought furniture locally, mostly in Lostwithiel itself, which is a hub of antique and vintage shops. As she describes it, "The whole ethos at the Duchy, guided by the then Duke of Cornwall, was to recycle, repair, and reuse, so the majority of the furniture I sourced was of a certain age." The same applied to most of the art, although Annabel commissioned the very talented George Young, who had studied at Falmouth, to paint a series of pictures of local areas, which are hung throughout the house.

It was a delicate balancing act decorating the house for both private and commercial use. "I had to keep in mind constantly that, for most of the time, the houses would be rented out," says Annabel, "and therefore practicality was very important, trying to make rooms as bombproof as possible, as there would be a constant stream of children. But I was also trying to retain the elegance of the house at the same time, so that the Duke of Cornwall felt at home when he was staying. I hope I succeeded!" She certainly did. The manor, as we found it, was graceful but not grand, and both practical and pretty. From the bespoke willow-green Cornishware in the kitchen, to the squidgy sofas strewn with blankets, to the antique dressers filled with pottery, to the open fire in the

sitting room surrounded by a tapestry-covered club fender, the entire house feels supremely comfortable and charmingly full of life.

When the battle-hardened Black Prince first visited Restormel Castle in 1354, one might presume he was gratified by the palatial fortress that he found. Restormel Manor might not be as outwardly impressive as the imposing castle above it, but, in gentler times, it is undoubtedly fit for a modern Cornish duke.

A seventeenth-century farmhouse remodelled in the eighteenth century as a Strawberry Hill Gothic–style mansion

**LEFT:** The antiques in the sitting room were all sourced locally from Lostwithiel. The sofa is from Sofa.com.

**BELOW LEFT:** The sitting room is painted with Rain Lake by Sanderson. The sofa is from George Sherlock and is covered with a vintage blanket.

**OPPOSITE:** From the sitting room looking out to the hall. The curtains in the sitting room were made from antique sheets.

**ABOVE:** The dining room seats eighteen. The table and chairs are from OKA. The antique mirror was bought locally.

**RIGHT:** An antique dresser (sourced locally) filled with cabbageware. The crockery on the table carries the Duchy of Cornwall crest.

**OPPOSITE:** The wallpaper in the dining room is Egerton by Cole & Son.

**ABOVE:** The entrance to the kitchen in the manor house is hung with a collection of Spy prints.

**LEFT:** Bespoke Duchy of Cornwall Cornishware in a willow-green colour

**OPPOSITE:** The sitting room of the Trinity wing of the house has vintage Bennison curtains, an antique Ferahan rug, and a sofa from Sofa.com.

**ABOVE:** This bedroom is known as Sweet Pea, after its wallpaper by Cole & Son.

**OPPOSITE ABOVE AND BELOW:** Vintage coronation cups in a bedroom in Trinity. The curtains are by Volga Linen in a Parma grey stripe.

# Ropehawn
## *A private harbour*

There is no easy or conventional way of getting to Ropehawn. The most comfortable is to persuade its owner to pick you up in a boat from the charming Georgian harbour of Charlestown and ferry you two miles across the pristine waters of St. Austell Bay to the house's private dock. The only other access is by foot and involves dropping down off the South West Coast Path and a ten-minute scramble through woodland along a vertiginous rock-strewn trail. Both journeys add to the adventurous spirit of the place, and you are amply rewarded for your efforts to get there by the secluded paradise that awaits you.

Ropehawn was originally a base for the netting and curing of pilchards. For more than 350 years it was owned and managed by the Hext family, who eventually, at the turn of the twentieth century, converted it from a fishing outpost into a family home. They completely reconstructed the house and, unusually, were able to buy the foreshore from the Duchy of Cornwall, making it one of the very few houses on the South Coast to have its own private harbour. In 1989, the Hexts sold it to Rex Turner, a retired naval commander, who spent huge energy rebuilding the seawalls, not to mention installing a pair of cannons above the slipway. It now belongs to Christopher and Harriet Casey and their children, Isla, Sholto, and Pip. The Caseys bought Ropehawn fourteen years ago, having spotted it in *The Week* magazine. Moving in involved transporting everything from Charlestown by an inflatable raft towed behind a boat. Absolutely everything arrived by sea, from beds, sofas, and fridges to the oak trees that were used in the landscaping of the property. Christopher even shipped in a pair of giant mechanical diggers on an old military landing craft to continue with the reconstruction of the "rock armour" of the harbour.

Until as late as the 1970s, the house had no water. The ancient well in the garden had produced only "brackish water" for centuries. So, on a practically daily basis, the owners used to have to take a boat a few hundred yards down the coastline to a spring of freshwater dribbling from a rock above a sandy

Ropehawn at high tide. The house sits directly above its private harbour.

cove, and fill barrels with water for the house. "I don't suppose much washing was done in those days," muses Christopher. The four-bedroom house is much more comfortable nowadays. The dining room (which leads through to a galley kitchen) is the centre of the house. With its wooden rafters and huge bay window framing a perfect sea view, it has the feeling of a stateroom on a full-rigged galleon. This is where the family congregates to plan the day's escapades, sitting round an antique kitchen table that came with the house. Sixteen-year-old Isla fancifully claims that "it was cut from an oak that Henry VIII lay under as a young boy." At one end of the room is a traditional Cornish range built in Wadebridge in the mid-nineteenth century. "We thought of taking it out," says Harriet, "but it's a piece of history, and it is also probably holding the house up!" Directly below the house is a walled garden that provides a sheltered space for outdoor eating. It used to be a large, roofed building that was used for the salting and packing of the pilchards before they were hauled up the hill. The walls have holes in them for the timbers from which fishing nets would be hung to dry. Just beyond, standing proudly above the water's edge, is the Sea Room. This was originally an Edwardian garden room built by the Hexts, which has now been converted into a one-bedroom guesthouse.

Life at Ropehawn is exceedingly "Swallows and Amazons" (after the 1930s children's adventure novel by Arthur Ransome). The children love to head off for adventures on the water. They take their kayaks or paddleboards to visit the otherwise inaccessible coves of the bay. They rarely bump into other humans but often come across seals or find themselves accompanied by pods of dolphins. They like to explore the caves of Silvermine Beach, which, for centuries, were used by smugglers to hide barrels of tea, tobacco, and brandy. Christopher and his sons are also keen fishermen. They cast their lines off the rocks for sea bass or take a boat out for mackerel. They also keep a couple of lobster pots offshore, which they bait with mackerel heads. Christopher oversees the cooking of what they catch. He often prepares bass as ceviche and usually boils the lobsters in "a whacking great pan." The girls get quite squeamish when they hear the lobsters scrabbling about, so sometimes, instead, he dispatches them quickly by cleaving them in two and putting them on the BBQ. The bay is full of rope-grown mussels, which the whole family adore. They are particularly delicious, as horseshoe-shaped St. Austell Bay is home to some of the cleanest seawater in Europe. In 2023, an eight-hundred-acre seagrass meadow was discovered just out to sea. Divers have since discovered all manner of rare species living there, from short-snouted seahorses to broad-nosed pipefish and curled octopus. It is a marine heaven, and it explains why the waters of the bay are almost uncannily clear.

Swimming in the mouth of the harbour

The Caseys make good use of *Finlandia*, their traditional wooden fishing boat. It was built in Looe in 1962 by the boat maker Curtis and Pape. They take it across the bay to their favourite restaurant, Sam's, on the pretty beach of Polkerris, or on to the bustling harbour of Fowey thirty minutes away. Directly across from Ropehawn, but hidden in a wooded valley, is Menabilly House—for twenty-five years the home of Daphne du Maurier. It is said that the great Cornish novelist used Ropehawn as her inspiration for the boathouse in *Rebecca*.

The Caseys are no strangers to adventure. The whole family rides: Christopher hunts and is former field master of the Beaufort, and the children all play polo. What is more, the Caseys own a 1921 wooden sailing trawler, which they keep in La Rochelle and use to explore the islands of the French Atlantic coast, living on it for weeks at a time. The eighty-foot boat is a unique example of a French-owned Dunkirk Little Ship that was pressed into action during the evacuation of Allied troops from France in 1940.

A skull-and-crossbones flag flutters at the entrance to Ropehawn's harbour. It was left by a guest earlier in the summer. Christopher has kept it up, as "it's actually quite useful to know where the wind is coming from." But I also suspect that this family of pirates doesn't mind the rakish air it gives the place.

**ABOVE:** The dining room leads through to the galley kitchen. The antique Cornish range, made in Wadebridge, has been in the house since the nineteenth century. The prints above it come from Hooper & Shaw, an art gallery in Newquay.

**LEFT:** The antique oak table in the dining room with chairs from Vincent Sheppard. The mirror came from Lorfords Antiques in Tetbury, and the big pendant lights from a vintage shop in nearby Fowey. The balloons are left over from Pip's birthday party.

**OPPOSITE:** Pip making good use of the window seat in the bay window of the dining room

THE BOOK OF TIDES

**ABOVE:** The circular games table came from Harriet's grandmother. The lamp bears Harriet's family crest. The sofas are from Ikea. The windswept tree drawings in the bookcase are by Nicole Heidaripour.

**OPPOSITE ABOVE:** Isla's bedroom with majestic views across St. Austell Bay

**OPPOSITE BELOW:** A guest bedroom with a collection of paintings from France

**ABOVE:** A door in the walled garden leads directly onto the quayside and Ropehawn's private harbour.

**RIGHT:** The cannons, looking out to Gribbin Head, were left by previous owner Rex Turner, a retired naval commander.

**OPPOSITE:** Lunch in the walled garden. This was originally a roofed building used for curing and packing pilchards.

# The Fable
## *A fairy-tale cottage*

The Fable, quite simply, looks good enough to eat. The cottage is so named because it might well have fallen from the pages of a children's book—most obviously the tale of Hansel and Gretel by the Brothers Grimm. Its delicious, two-foot-thick, undulating walls resemble the royal icing on a wedding cake, and its chimney stacks bulge curvaceously like marshmallows. Its overhanging roof looks hewn from great slabs of gingerbread. The sugar-pink windows below are painted in peach blossom, and planted all around are flowering red currants, wild strawberries, and heavily scented roses. It is the most edible-looking house we have ever come across.

But, in fact, the walls of this late seventeenth-century cottage are made not of sugar and egg white but of painted rubble and cob, and its roof is not gingerbread but combed wheat reed thatch. Cob buildings, which are typically thatched, can be found across Cornwall and are recognisable by their thick, lime-washed walls and tiny windows and their painted rubble stack chimneys. Cob is an ancient and traditional Cornish building material. It is made by mixing mud or clay with chopped straw and gravel-like "shilf," which is the name given to little pieces of waste slate. Water was added, and it was trodden down into a workable mixture by humans, horses, or oxen. If cattle were involved, then dung invariably ended up in the mix as well. And if horses did the treading, then their long hairs added to the binding. The cob was then laid, layer upon layer, to create the thick walls of these dwellings—generally twenty-four inches thick, with deep-set windows that provide cottages such as these with excellent thermal mass, keeping them warm in winter and cool in summer.

The Fable can be found in the tiny hamlet of Ventongimps, near Callestick, Perranporth, which sounds like the address of one of J. R. R. Tolkien's hobbits. The front door knocker is of a pixie sitting on a toadstool, which adds to the cottage's fairy-tale charm. A quick rap brings Sarah Stanley, the Fable's owner, to the door. Sarah welcomes us into the home that she shares with her daughter, Morgane, and her Jack Russell, Ruby. Ruby, unlike many of her breed, "is not

The Fable, with its cob walls and thatched roof

a natural troublemaker" but a calm and gentle-natured terrier with a floppy ear that hangs down, coquettishly, over her right eye.

Sarah is Cornish, born and bred. She grew up on her parents' farm in a tiny hamlet between Newquay and Padstow. As a child, Sarah was keen to help out, feeding the animals and eventually driving tractors. After school she went to agricultural college but then changed tack and trained as a chef. After working at restaurants in London, she spent twelve years travelling and working abroad in Africa, India, and Australia, where her children were born. Eventually, missing home, and having an opportunity to convert a barn on her family farm, she moved back to Cornwall. Sarah then set up a company called Unique Homestays, originally as a service for putting up students and backpackers with Cornish families. But then she reckoned surely some vacationers would rather stay in a beautiful family home than in a hotel. She was right, and people were charmed by the quirkiness and originality of the houses that Sarah found for them to rent. Twenty years later and Sarah now manages more than seventy rental properties in Cornwall with a business that employs dozens of local people.

Sarah bought the Fable for herself and Morgane a decade ago but now rents it out part-time through Unique Homestays. She fell in love with it the moment she saw it because of its cute character and its cob walls. Sarah loves their enveloping thickness, which is particularly obvious in the sitting room and makes the cottage seem extraordinarily cosy.

The front door opens straight onto that sitting room, which is the earliest part of the house. The Fable was originally a dairy, and an antique milk churn in the corner of the fireplace is a nod to its history. The walls are painted in Dulux Porcelain Doll matte white, and, as in all the rooms in the house, Sarah has created a simple and relaxed feel. She loves recycling old furniture and fittings, and searching the county and beyond for vintage pieces is one of her passions. She likes things that are a bit distressed and have a sense of a life already lived. Baskets of kindling, fairy lights, and dried flowers add an air of cottagey cosiness.

Sarah considers the kitchen to be the most important room in the house. It has the same relaxed, pared-back attitude as the rest of the cottage, with white, purposely distressed floorboards, and mismatched wooden chairs around a farmhouse table. Sarah modestly describes herself as "a basic farmhouse cook" despite having worked as a chef. She does, however, admit to making a "mean Cornish pasty—although not as good as my mum's." Sarah likes to cook the food of her childhood, like big stews with dumplings, made on the AGA and served with homegrown vegetables. Hearty farmhouse fare appropriate for a family

Sarah and her daughter, Morgane, outside the Fable

that has been working outside all day in mixed Cornish weather. As a child she would always have high tea at four o'clock. Egg and bacon pie, cakes, "lemon solid," and home-baked bread with locally churned butter and honeycomb. And to this day, Sarah's mother's pantry is always full of cakes (made with her own duck eggs): caraway-seed drop buns, ginger cake, saffron loaves, lemon drizzle cake, and Victoria sponges. Our mouths water as she describes it all.

Sarah is a keen gardener. Surrounding the cottage are willow trees, carnelians, and holly bushes, along with privet topiary in galvanised pots. And everywhere there are roses: wonderful-smelling peach-coloured roses, pink rambling roses, and red climbing roses, all from the Cornish Rose Company in Mitchell. As we leave this magical cottage, we notice the blue flowers in a pot by the front door. They are forget-me-nots, as if we ever could.

**ABOVE:** In the sitting room, Sarah put in a wood-burning stove next to the ancient shepherd's seat with a slate top. A milk churn reflects the dairy origins of the cottage. The chest is full of board games.

**RIGHT:** Sarah fell in love with the texture and thickness of the plastered cob walls.

**OPPOSITE:** The desk end of the sitting room—which is full of vintage finds from antique, charity, and retro shops all over Cornwall.

**ABOVE:** Ruby, the floppy-eared Jack Russell, in the kitchen of the Fable. She is sitting on a hessian cushion on top of an original stone bench.

**OPPOSITE ABOVE:** Myrtle blossom on the kitchen table—a symbol of romantic love. The linen tablecloth and plates are from the White Company.

**OPPOSITE BELOW:** The distressed blue dresser in the kitchen is an Indian piece from the Antique Village, a huge antiques, vintage, retro, and salvage centre near Exeter in Devon.

8

Est 1908
Tel 246
by

**LEFT:** Sarah's bed, dressed in bedding from the White Company. Her bedroom, like the rest of the cottage, is full of vintage finds, including lights made from jam jars.

**BELOW LEFT:** A clawfoot bath with nickel taps. A ceramic-tiled, wood-effect floor. Lights from the Garden Trading company are on either side of a circular mirror.

**OPPOSITE:** A butler's sink in the kitchen

LLOYD'S
SIGNAL STATION

# The Signal Station
## *A converted beacon*

The Lizard Peninsula is the most southerly point in Great Britain and one of Cornwall's most rugged and unspoilt corners. It is where the Atlantic Ocean turns into the English Channel, and it is the first place in the United Kingdom that a ship crossing the ocean from the Americas will hit. The first building they would likely see is the iconic Lloyd's Signal Station, a castellated, foursquare white block in a commanding clifftop setting on Bass Point.

The Signal Station was built in 1872 by Fox and Company Shipping Agents as a communication hub for passing vessels, with its officers using flags to message them, connecting with London via telegraph. Within five years, the Lizard station was being used by more than one thousand ships per month, and in 1883, Lloyd's of London took over the operation of the station and stencilled its name on the side of the building. Communication between the station and vessels was mostly via flag semaphore. Ships as much as eight miles out to sea would use telescopes to see a series of pennants fluttering on guy ropes at the top of the station. Occasionally at night (and in poor weather) coloured lights, rockets, guns, or even steam whistles were used as well. The nearby Marconi Wireless Station and the invention of radio eventually rendered the Signal Station obsolete; the building ceased all operations in 1969 and was subsequently bought by the National Trust.

The Signal Station also acted as a navigational point. Ships would line up red markers on the building and use them to avoid the treacherous "Rogue Rock" not far off Bass Point. The Lizard Peninsula is one of the most dangerous coastlines in the British Isles and is historically known as "the Graveyard of Ships" because there have been more shipwrecks per square mile off this headland than any other part of Britain.

Lloyd's Signal Station was bought, on a leasehold from the National Trust, by James and Anna Reader in 2018. The couple share a fascination with the British coastline and are gripped by unusual coastal properties. They also own a unique house on Luskentyre Bay on the Isle of Harris in the Hebrides

Lloyd's Signal Station, built in 1872, sits "like a giant sugar cube" on top of Bass Point.

(which is the most westerly point in the United Kingdom). James had always holidayed in Cornwall and vividly remembers attending an air show at Royal Navy Air Station Culdrose (also known as HMS Seahawk) as a young boy. It was a formative experience and fostered in him a love for both South Cornwall and aviation.

Anna has Cornish roots. Her father was a seaman who joined the merchant navy as a sixteen-year-old. On returning from his epic first voyage and heading to Falmouth, he recalls sailing past Lizard Point and seeing Lloyd's Signal Station "like a castle on a hill." He is now a maritime historian and has helped James and Anna research the building.

The Readers first came to see it on a crisp winter's day. All the way along the drive from the village of Lizard, they could see its dominating presence on the skyline—"like a giant sugar cube," says James. Its solid, plastered walls are several feet thick and built to survive the worst storms. In very serious weather, near neighbours used to gather there to take shelter. As soon as they arrived, the Readers were mesmerised by its panoramic sea views and gripped by its sense of history.

It was somewhat shabby when they bought it. There were cheap Formica surfaces in the kitchen and horrid lilac carpets upstairs. The Readers quickly got to work and decorated it with whitewashed walls and soft blues and greys that don't distract from the incredible views and constantly changing colours of the "kaleidoscopic" sea beyond. A chintzy, cottagecore vibe would have seemed somehow inappropriate. On the ground floor, which originally housed the telegraph rooms, they used industrial fittings to reflect the utilitarian nature of this vital shipping beacon. But the house is not without luxury. The bedrooms, including one with a four-poster bed, are elegant and there is a beautifully appointed wet room on the first floor. On the top floor, where the signallers used to work, the couple have built a stunning "crow's nest" bar which leads onto the roof terrace where Anna likes to do yoga at daybreak in the summer months. Throughout the house, the Readers have paid homage to the history of the building with a collection of signalling artefacts, vintage postcards, pictures of wrecks, and antiquarian books related to the maritime history of Cornwall.

The house has borne witness to extraordinary events over the years. The multitude of shipwrecks directly off the coast here included that of the passenger liner SS *Suevic* in 1907, leading to the biggest lifeboat rescue in British history when Royal National Lifeboat Institution volunteers battled high winds to save 456 souls, including 70 babies. On the 10th of April, 1912, watchers at the Signal Station were the last people on the British mainland to see the *Titanic* as it passed by on its fateful first voyage. Five days later the Marconi

hut, a few hundred yards away, was the first place to receive the sinking ship's SOS message. In 1936, people gathered on the clifftop in amazement to see the *Hindenburg Zeppelin* fly over Bass Point en route to America. In World War II (which the Signal Station spent draped in camouflage netting), signalmen watched dogfights between British and Nazi fighter planes take place in the skies above them.

It is still a dramatic place to live. There is constant sea traffic on this busy shipping lane, and patrolling coast guard helicopters compete for one's attention with the sea life that can be spotted from the house, including seals, dolphins, and all manner of rare seabirds. But more gripping than anything else is the weather. When storms roll in from the Atlantic, it feels unbelievably elemental, and the Readers are thankful for the house's three-foot-thick walls and glad that they are not responsible for signalling ships from its roof.

Anna, James, and three-year-old Arlo enjoying a Cornish cream tea in the garden. The slate table and benches are cut into the hillside above an old gun emplacement. Lizard Lighthouse is in the background.

**OPPOSITE ABOVE:** Lorna Doone—an English show cocker spaniel—in the bay window of the dining room

**OPPOSITE BELOW:** The sitting room is decorated with antique maps, a barometer, and a vintage life ring—all items found in local haunts, including a reclamation centre in Penzance wonderfully named Shiver Me Timbers.

**RIGHT:** Hanging on the wall of the first-floor study are a collection of semaphore flags. This room would have originally been the telegraph office.

**ABOVE:** The black chest of drawers came from Ardingly Antiques Fair. The rope doorstop on top of it came from a shop in Cadgwith Cove. Hanging above are a series of framed postcards featuring local shipwrecks.

**ABOVE RIGHT:** The dressing table and chair came from OKA. The ceiling lamp is from Nkuku.

Herringbone tiles behind a circular mirror in the wet room

**ABOVE:** Industrial lights above the kitchen island, which was designed and built by Cornish Kitchens and Bathrooms.

**OPPOSITE:** The dining end of the open-plan kitchen. The table and chairs are from Swoon Editions. The ceiling light was made by Anna with driftwood purchased from Shiver Me Timbers in Penzance.

HAMES TRADING CO

**ABOVE:** The Signal Station from the Coast Path

**OPPOSITE ABOVE:** The view westwards from the Signal Station towards Lizard Lighthouse

**OPPOSITE BELOW:** The roof of the Signal Station, from where the semaphore flags would be flown. Anna likes to do yoga there on summer mornings.

# Point Neptune House
## *An Italianate villa*

"Last night I dreamt I went to Manderley again." So begins *Rebecca*, the most famous of all Daphne du Maurier's novels. The secretive mansion of Manderley, which lies at the heart of the book, was largely inspired by the Cornish house that du Maurier leased and lived in for twenty-five years—Menabilly, an early Georgian manor house built on Elizabethan foundations, hidden in woodland behind Fowey. The Menabilly estate has been owned by the Rashleigh family since they first settled in Fowey in the sixteenth century. The Rashleighs were prolific merchants and shipowners who, by astutely buying land during the dissolution of the monasteries, went on to become one of the wealthiest and most influential families in Cornwall. In 1855, William Rashleigh inherited Menabilly along with a thirty-thousand-acre estate that made him the largest landowner in Cornwall. William was an adventurous young man who travelled extensively through Europe, Turkey, the Holy Land, and Egypt before serving in the Royal Navy during the Crimean War. He had a deep love for the sea, and when he returned to Cornwall, he decided that he didn't want to live away from the shoreline, in the elegant and discreet confines of Menabilly, but as close to the sea as he possibly could and in the house of his dreams. And so, in 1864, he built Point Neptune.

Point Neptune House sits on a clifftop above St. Catherine's Cove, overlooking the mouth of the River Fowey. It is built on the site of an old Napoleonic gun emplacement that stood guard over Fowey Harbour. It was created as an Italianate villa—a picturesque version of classical architecture inspired by the Italian Renaissance, with adjoining arched windows and prominently bracketed cornicing on towers based on Italian campanili and belvederes. But while it summons the spirit of the Italian Riviera, it is solidly built of coursed slate with granite dressings to survive the battering of Cornish winter storms. The building rests on granite buttresses that appear to rise straight from the sea and the whole house is oriented towards the water. Short of living on a boat, William couldn't have built himself a home more connected to the sea.

Point Neptune is now home to the scientist and biotech entrepreneur Professor Sir Christopher Evans and his wife, Lady Anne. The couple had been

The east façade of Point Neptune House, built in 1864

The kitchen terrace looking out to sea and the English Channel

looking, for some time, for a coastal home—to be a refuge from Sir Christopher's extraordinarily busy working life and a place to be with their family. And they wanted something special. "With our background in fine arts, we were hoping to find a property with historical integrity and presence," says Lady Anne. The couple felt an immediate connection to the house as soon as they walked in. "We fell instantly in love and just knew we had to have it. We feel extremely privileged to have found it and are now able to safeguard it for future generations."

Living in the house feels rather like being at sea. The creaking wooden floors and glazing of the lantern room are reminiscent of a man-of-war's stateroom. And with almost every room in the house giving views directly over the sea, you get the impression of being aboard a majestic galleon. When it came to decorating the house, Lady Anne embraced the maritime feel and there are nautical details throughout. The house is full of exquisite shellwork, pieces of coral, and antique model boats. There are various references to Neptune, the great Roman sea god, including the front door knocker showing him astride a pair of dolphins. The spectacular lantern room in the centre of the house is used as a dining hall with magnificent hand-painted de Gournay wallpaper depicting Captain Cook's discovery of the Pacific Islands aboard HMS *Endeavour*. But the house is also a showcase for the Evanses' impressive collection of, amongst other things, mid-century English and European furniture and Art Deco, modern, and contemporary art. There is an especial emphasis on Cornish art across all mediums, including paintings by Ben Nicholson, Patrick Heron, Sandra Blow, Fred Yates, Wilhelmina Barns-Graham, and others.

The house is surrounded by beautiful terraced gardens. Lady Anne is a passionate gardener and plantswoman, and a trained landscape designer. She has filled the beds with subtropical plants and coastal species that thrive in exposed conditions: Torbay palms, Yucca recurvifolia, cycads, Pinus mugo, Camearops humilis, agave, and so on. As the sun moves round the house, the Evanses use different seating areas, including a lawned terrace overlooking St. Catherine's Cove. "I love the sound of activity and children playing on the beach," says Lady Anne, "and watching the swimmers who are there every day of the year regardless of the weather." One of the Evanses' daughters, Amy, can also often be found in the sea, even in the depths of winter, swimming off a strip of private pebbled beach directly below the house.

The family love to walk into Fowey. This ancient port town (whose parish church was established in the seventh century) is full of great shops, restaurants, and pubs, including the Ship Inn, which the first Rashleighs to come to the area used to live in. But most of all they like to be at the house watching the to-ing and fro-ing of boats in the harbour. They always make sure they are there for the Royal Regatta week in August, when the estuary is teeming with colourful

sailboats. But for Anne, "the house is just as appealing in the off-season, as I love the sense of raw nature that you get with winter storms." She relishes curling up with a book in the drawing room whilst the rain thrashes against the windows. Du Maurier is one of her favourite authors. "But whereas Rebecca might have dreamt of Manderley, on returning from my last stay in Fowey, I dreamt, vividly, of Point Neptune House." We can understand why. This was the last house that we visited on our tour of Cornwall and a fitting one to end with. Of all the houses that we saw on our wonderful adventure in the Delectable Duchy, this was arguably the most spectacular. William Rashleigh knew what he was doing when he built it.

Sir Christopher and Lady Anne Evans at the Italianate villa of Point Neptune House

Diamond

Lady Anne designed the drawing room to create a functional immersive experience, as if walking into and becoming part of a Ben Nicholson painting, in terms of structure, texture, colour, and scale. The carpet is based on a small painting by Nicholson, which literally grounds the space.

**LEFT:** The boot room is painted Stiffkey Blue by Farrow & Ball and accented with Poseidon wallpaper by Pierre Frey.

**OPPOSITE:** The kitchen table, with a glimpse of the Lantern Room beyond

The dining hall is lit by a lantern ceiling and a chandelier made from mussel shells.

The primary bedroom leading into the bathroom. The picture, by Fred Yates, was painted when he visited and stayed at Point Neptune. The previous owner kindly allowed the Evanses to buy it so it could stay with the house.

The primary bedroom is painted Berrington Blue by Farrow & Ball. The bedhead is an image from J. W. Waterhouse's *Miranda*.

**ABOVE:** This single bedroom has fantastic views towards the harbour. It is wallpapered in Bonne Peche by Pierre Frey—inspired by fish market stalls with their fish, shellfish, and crustaceans.

**OPPOSITE:** The desk in the drawing room. The views directly over and out to sea make you feel as if you are on the bridge of a ship.

**LEFT:** The panelled first-floor hallway is painted Dix Blue by Farrow & Ball.

**OPPOSITE:** The front of Point Neptune House, which was built in an Italianate villa style in 1864. The adjoining arched windows and prominently bracketed cornicing are typical of this architectural style.

# ACKNOWLEDGEMENTS

Milo, Mark, and I spent the first night of our journey around Cornwall at Jamaica Inn, on a high and remote spot in the middle of Bodmin Moor. Opened in 1750, this coaching inn became famous as the backdrop and title of Daphne du Maurier's bestselling novel *Jamaica Inn*: a dastardly tale of murderous shipwreckers and smugglers. Despite it being early spring, we arrived amidst a terrible storm and had to sprint from the car before sitting, sodden and shivering, before the fire. It seemed like an ill omen, and that night, as the wind and rain battered the windows, we wondered what we had let ourselves in for. Cornwall can be a wild and forbidding place, and during that sleepless night we felt a long way from the gentle joys of the bucolic Cotswolds.

But by the morning the storm had abated, the mist had cleared, and we headed west in bright sunshine. The landscape that unfolded before us was breathtaking. We soon crossed the river Camel, which takes its name from the old Cornish for "crooked river," and followed its winding path to the ancient fishing village of Padstow to photograph our first house. That evening we crossed the Camel estuary on a ferry to have dinner in Rock, where we feasted on oysters, mussels, and megrim sole, all gathered and caught from the waters directly in front of us. We drank a delicate pink sparkling wine, scented with strawberries, made by the Camel Valley Vineyard just a few miles inland, and toasted the adventures to come. The misery of the previous night already seemed a distant memory. What followed were some of the most pleasurable working weeks of our lives as we travelled the length and breadth of the Delectable Duchy, taking in its spectacular scenery and visiting some of its most beautiful houses. By the end of the journey, we were sun-kissed, windswept, and fat (thanks to an endless succession of clotted cream teas) but full of love for this wonderful county and gratitude for the kindness of its inhabitants.

To all those who graciously allowed us into their homes, and to those who acted as tour guides, introduced us to houses, and provided those fattening cream teas, we are supremely grateful.

Ferryside, on the Fowey Estuary, the onetime home of author Daphne du Maurier. It was originally built in the 1800s as a shipwright's workshop.

**ABOVE:** Tintagel Old Post Office—a fourteenth-century stone house built to the plan of a medieval manor house

**OPPOSITE:** Doyden Castle, near Port Isaac. A neo-gothic folly built around 1830 as gambling bolthole and party house by Samuel Symons. Now owned by the National Trust

We would particularly like to thank Josephine Ashby, Lorna Badham-Borg, Erskine Berry, Leonora Birts, Edward Bulmer, John and Shellard Campbell, Fred Cartwright, Christopher Casey, Grania Cavendish, Nina Chinn, Lindsay Cuthill, David Du Croz, Anthony Draper, Tremayne Carew Pole, Claire Coode, Emma Cooper-Key, Pandora Cooper-Key, Mary-Ann Cooksey, Henrietta Courtauld, Jonathon Cunliffe, Emma Dean, Ruth and Guy East, Annabel Elliot, Stuart Ellis, Christopher and Anne Evans, Bianca Fincham, Christian Fleming, Elizabeth Fortescue, Sarah Fortescue, Peter Gain, Alice Gates, Fiona Golfar, Gavin and Clare Green, Martin and Amanda Hedley, Charlotte Henderson, Caryn Hibbert, Suzy Hoodless, Ali Hope, Alice Irwin, Alice Johnson, Hannah Jones, Rob Kendall, Kate Leigh-Wood, Phyllida Lloyd, Sarah Lowther, Tanya Lutyens, Kim and Tina Oxenham, Kate Packenham, Hannah Pascoe, Sarah Percy-Davis, Nick and Martha Prideaux-Brune, Anna Reader, Karl Taylor, Evie Sykes, Stephen Smyth-Tyrrell, Nigel Stacey, Sarah Stanley, Claire Vickers, Harold van Lier, Claire Vickers, and Sarah Welch.

As always, we would like to thank our amazing editorial team and publishers at Abrams in New York, in particular Shawna Mullen, and everyone at Abrams & Chronicle Books in London.

Editor: Shawna Mullen
Designer: Darilyn Lowe Carnes
Managing Editor: Lisa Silverman
Production Manager: Larry Pekarek

Library of Congress Control Number: 2025941927

ISBN: 978-1-4197-7381-5
eISBN: 979-8-88707-291-3

Text copyright © 2026 Milo Campbell and Katy Campbell
Photographs copyright © 2026 Mark Nicholson

Jacket and cover © 2026 Abrams

Published in 2026 by Abrams, an imprint of ABRAMS. All rights reserved. No portion of this book may be reproduced, stored in a retrieval system, or transmitted in any form or by any means, mechanical, electronic, photocopying, recording, or otherwise, without written permission from the publisher.

Printed and bound in China
10 9 8 7 6 5 4 3 2 1

Abrams books are available at special discounts when purchased in quantity for premiums and promotions as well as fundraising or educational use. Special editions can also be created to specification. For details, contact specialsales@abramsbooks.com or the address below.

Abrams® is a registered trademark of Harry N. Abrams, Inc.

**ABRAMS** The Art of Books
195 Broadway, New York, NY 10007
abramsbooks.com

ABRAMS is represented in the UK and Europe by Abrams & Chronicle Books, 1 West Smithfield, London EC1A 9JU and Média Participations, 57 rue Gaston Tessier, 75166 Paris, France.
abramsandchronicle.co.uk and media-participations.com
info@abramsandchronicle.co.uk